Patagonia
the Camino Home

KATHARINE ELLIOTT
Bestselling Author of *A Camino of the Soul*

A Camino of the Soul – Book #2

Acknowledgements

Writing a book becomes, in the final stages, the project of a village. With love and thanks to my tribe:

Helen and Cheryl...you gather my words, sift, bless, send them back for review with love and tenderness. I love you my life-sisters.

Dawn, thank-you for your love and belief in me; for encouraging me to follow my soul calling.

Wendy Hall, my editor, once again you gently apply your skills and bring my work its finishing touches. I am blessed to have you on this journey.

Heidi Sutherlin, you are brilliant—truly brilliant with your cover designs and formatting. Thankyou!

For all who have helped in the launch process of this book, and you know who you are, I am forever grateful for your continued support in this process.

Lexy Ann, thank-you for sharing your love. We were meant to meet on this Patagonian journey, and I am blessed to have you in my life.

To the outstanding team at Say Hueque in Argentina—you were the perfect partners in my adventure.

And to my son Gregory and his beautiful bride Allison, you two are the best cheerleaders any Mom could hope to have and you are so truly and deeply loved!

Finally, Mary, my sister, your words of encouragement always seem to come at the precise moment I need them most. Who knew when you were born that the Universe was giving me the gift of a best friend as you entered this world as my sister? Gratitude...gratitude...gratitude. I love you.

DEDICATION

For Mom, whose unconditional love and brilliant creativity wove the threads of treasured memories and traditions through the tapestry of my life. I love you.

Your

Kathy-girl

TABLE OF CONTENTS

INTRODUCTION

On the rocky cliffs of Finisterre, in northwestern Spain, high above the crashing Atlantic Ocean, my soul spoke a truth I had known all along, a truth the Universe had been whispering: I must walk to this place, this ancient end of the earth, to walk away from him...to be able to start anew.

In the summer of 2011, when the first call to walk the Camino Santiago de Compostela had tugged at my soul, I would not have known this was my *why*. A tug so fierce I had no choice but to follow, the next years would guide me to an understanding of the energies of the Universe in action. I would learn the importance of gratitude in our ability to co-conspire with the Universe. I would learn the marvels of synchronicities, the guidance that is ours if we simply listen. Angel messages would become an expected part of daily life—always welcome, never a surprise.

My deceased mother-in-law, Sis, challenged me to look deeply at issues I might be contemplating by alerting me with her signals from beyond: 11s; 7:11 on a clock face, 111 on a license plate, 6:11, 5:11...she jolted me with her message, "You are on the right track; keep following your heart, all will be well."

My Aunt Mary Jo, taken at age fifty-nine from complications with multiple sclerosis, had sat close on my bedside one lazy Rovinj afternoon, comforting and assuring me that financial issues burdening my spirit were not really issues at all. Her energy whispering to my heart that I need not be concerned. All was in order. Everything would be all right.

The spirits of my grandparents, both having died years earlier, joining me on a rocky promontory as I silently sat in meditation above the waters of the Mediterranean Sea. Grandpa's applewood pipe tobacco essence swirling pungent in the moist wet air. Grandma's tender soft voice calling out to me in love and affection, "Katy, Katy, my love" as she had all the years we shared. Angel messages—I have been blessed.

Air, fresh and clean, caressed my face on the cliffs of Finisterre. The sun shone warm on my skin on the day I reached the lighthouse at the ancient end of the world. On the horizon, a new life beckoned. My spirit had grown. My soul had spoken over the last years; particularly these last six weeks of trekking the five hundred miles from St Jean Pied de Port in the French Pyrenees, over the mountains into northern Spain, and then west to the Atlantic Ocean. The walk was a lesson in trusting...a lesson in listening to the whisperings of the Universe. Nothing in my life is out of order. That my Camino would actually begin only months after the word divorce was spoken seemed written in the stars. Three years in the making; a walk planned then replanned at least twice, had occurred exactly when it was meant—exactly when I would need the solitude most. I had followed the call and in doing so had been reborn.

That final evening in Finisterre, only two days of walking remained in my journey. Settled on the small terrace of my chosen

B&B, I watched the tiny fishing boats bob in the calm harbor waters.

Reading my journaling, soaking in words I had written over the last six weeks, I sat in wonder all that had occurred.

Words which had flowed from pen to paper since that glorious morning outside Pamplona when my deceased sister Jeannie, an angel guide in my life, came to me speaking quietly to my heart.

Her message had been simple, direct, and passionate:

"Start writing...don't ask what or why...just start."

Shocked at the clarity of her voice, the energy of her presence in the midst of newly harvested Spanish fields, she spoke direct instructions deep into my soul. Ruminating on her words, I smiled. Nothing, nothing in my life was out of order. Jeannie, now a being clear of time and space, an energy, free-flowing, had given me my purpose: "Start writing." She knew that this walk would bring me to a new understanding of my life purpose. That I did not yet comprehend the *how's and why's* was neither here nor there. My instructions were clear. Long-distance walking and writing were my purpose—my obligation in this physical life. A wall blocking my vision had been slowly torn down over the past six weeks. Sharply in focus, a bright new world lay before me.

Armed with an unquestionable belief that my life was moving forward as was intended, I let go of resistance and simply followed what my heart called me to do. A final two days of walking, finally laying down my now beloved trekking stick at Muxia, in northwestern Galicia, Spain.

Clarity. For now, I had done what I had come to do. It was time to return to the States after six years abroad and begin again: write a new chapter. It was time to walk away from Spain and all it had taught; walk away from Jack and the love we had once known, and move forward armed with the belief that when I set a clear intention, the Universe conspires with me to make it happen.

I now knew how to trust in the synchronicities of the Universe. My mantra of the last several years: I AM aware...I AM receptive...I AM accepting, would be my guiding mission statement.

It is time to go!

CHAPTER ONE

Leaving Spain!

"...And what is your intention?" asked the Universe.
"To follow my heart; to walk and write," stated a positive Me.

As the sun rises brilliant gold against a deep blue early morning haze, the sky is illuminated over my left shoulder, I am leaving Spain behind. Camino days have come to an end and with the final closure at Finisterre and Muxia, the realization that *home*, attempting to fit in and create some sort of new life, awaits me.

Nearing the end of the Camino, many pilgrims shared their angst at the thought of re-entering the hustle and bustle of their regular lives. It is a common fear; a trepidation known and discussed. A kind of *'post-Camino depression'* is not uncommon. Many take a few days before leaving the glories of this walk and find a hideaway to decompress. Spending time at The Little Fox

House in Muxia is a treat for many. Started by an ex-Camino-ite herself, it has become a haven for rest and reflection before reentering the world at large.

For me, decompression time will be a week in central California. A place of deep solitude where the ocean air will aid in keeping my currently uncluttered mind at peace. Several days of quiet contemplation—writing, walking, and sleeping long hours—will be my respite before heading home to Seattle...family...loved ones...activity.

I relish the time with my people, but first I must ensure my soul stays intact. This flight takes me west to San Francisco, and then I will drive south to Monterey where I will attempt to solidify what is next in my life. I know walking is a part. I know writing is paramount. Those commitments were made several days ago as I stood on the cliffs of Finisterre. Now, what to do with this soul knowledge?

The sky blazes over my left shoulder. I am keenly aware this is a start of a new day. A new chapter...a new life. Whatever I choose to call it. The past is past and what happens now is clothed in a mix of emotions.

The last few days in Spain have been a whirlwind of love and fun...laughter and tears. Goodbyes and "I'll be back soon," or "We will come to see you" promises. And a hug so tender between Jack and me that my heart broke. A snuggle with my sweet Lucky dog, my tears flowing on his soft wet nose. Those captivating brown eyes looking up at me.

But this too is part of the process of change and evolution in life. For me to grow and expand, to morph into all I can be, who and what I am supposed to be, this final goodbye had to occur as well. And I know this. I know this as sure as I know that pilgrimage walks will be my life and writing is now a calling. That psychological rocks will tumble in my way, and stumbles will happen, is a given. And, I will survive them all. These missteps are all leading to a new circle of love and life.

Where was it...the rock maze? A rock formation in a field along the Camino. Rocks placed side by side over time by individual pilgrims on their way toward Santiago. Circles forming, one outside the other, expanding, creating a maze at eye level. Yet, from the trail above, a divine clarity. All in order.

Just as my life and all of its happenings, one rock placed after another. Divine order. An intricate maze of people, places, loves lived and lost, each representative of a portion of my life...each a pebble in the maze. Yet, as I look back, all conspiring to work with me toward the next steps.

I am blessed to believe and trust that when I surrender and accept my life as it is, the Universe conspires to work with me toward my greatest dreams. Now, settled into my window seat for an eleven-hour flight to San Francisco, my heart knows all will be well. Decisions will be made; the right choices will show themselves. A new chapter awaits.

❋ ❋ ❋ ❋

Monterey

My time in Monterey has been a joyous and valuable break between the peace of the Camino and the ruckus of Seattle. I have had six days of decompression time to spend just as I imagined: sleep, walk, watch the fishing boats, listen to the screeching gulls and prehistoric looking pelicans as they flap and squawk overhead, meditate and plan for the future.

And, only a couple of weeks off the Camino, I have made plans for my next walk. It truly is quite amazing, and I find myself in awe of how it has all come together, but it has!

I hate the cold. Truly despise being cold. So, if I am going to go walking, it has to be in a warmer climate. And, since we are moving into winter in the northern hemisphere, it strikes me that southern is the place to be. Go find some summer, somewhere!

Australia and New Zealand sound enticing, but frankly, with a limited time schedule, it is just too far. In fact, with a time schedule of just less than three weeks, perhaps staying within the American continents makes sense.

Patagonia! Ever since I was in junior high school, pictures of Patagonia intrigued me. Partially the craggy granite mountain peaks, partially the thought of walking among penguins, Patagonia has called to my heart. And so, I start to research hikes and walks in southern Argentina and Chile. I will do this one alone. This is my proving ground for taking on the two thousand-kilometer Via Francigena within the next year or so. If I can manage this trek alone, I can certainly manage the VF, as it is known.

Two thousand kilometers from Canterbury in England to the Holy City of Rome, the pilgrimage route of the Via Francigena treks through northeastern France south toward Switzerland, across the Gran San Bernard Pass in the Alps and south into Italy. Winding through Tuscany, the path works its way to the heart of Christendom, the eternal city, Rome.

First chronicled in the tenth century by Archbishop Sigeric of Canterbury on his return walk from Rome to England, this route has been traveled by pilgrims for centuries. In modern day, it does not have the media attention that the Camino de Santiago has gained; nor is the infrastructure, in terms of accommodations and services, as plentiful. This is part of the draw.

The final certificate of completion for the Via Francigena has been given to approximately 30,000 pilgrims per year in the last two to three years versus the multitudes reaching numbers of 240,000 on the Camino de Santiago route.

The Via Francigena will be my next pilgrimage. I am shooting for summer of 2015. In the meantime, it is imperative I keep the momentum of walking and writing.

In these last couple of days, I have been researching hikes in Patagonia and have found my answer. I will travel to southern Argentina and spend four days hiking the trails of El Chaltén at the base of famed Mount Fitz Roy. From there I will take a bus into Chile and undertake the W Trek of Torres del Paine National Park. Named for its route, as it cuts in and out of glacial valleys, the W Trek is typically a five or six-day hike. I will overnight in refugios, fully outfitted trail huts, complete with meals and showers. I have never done much overnight camping and, quite frankly, the idea of carrying such gear is not my idea of a meditative adventure, although campgrounds for those heartier hikers are certainly available.

The W Trek, with its options, is perfect for me.

The only problem, February, when I have the time to go, is high season and with limited facilities, all accommodations must be booked in advance. The question: take on this booking challenge solo or work through a qualified agency and let them handle the details? Europe I know; South America is another realm. I have done a fair amount of traveling in these last years, but nothing that compares to this. This is out of my element.

Although I know where I wish to wander, I am in a quandary about the logistics. I have sent emails to agencies specializing in this hike, but as of last night, there have been no responses in forty-eight hours. What to do?

I believe the Universe works in amazing ways. I believe in synchronicity and although I understand personal choice and responsibility, I also know that when we watch, listen, trust— use our multisensory capabilities—a whole new world of information and communication opens up to us.

This morning, as I sat contemplating my potential trek to the mountains of Patagonia, trying to decide if I should spend the money on a self-guided tour coordinated by an agency or simply attempt to handle the logistics myself, I meditated. Clearly and distinctly I asked the Universe to point the way; show me an answer to this question. Shall I organize this myself or opt for an agency to help?

Almost immediately, as I was completing my morning meditation, an email popped up. I heard the notification ping as it pulled me from my quiet place a bit soon. The email was from the travel agent who I had been hoping to reach at Say Hueque Tours in Argentina. The agent who "happened to be working today," as he said, was asking if I was still considering my trip. This was the travel agent who normally does not go into the office on a Sunday, but had seen my last email and decided it was time to respond. Synchronicity.

As I read his message and responded with my own, I caught sight of the clock face: 7:11 AM; my energy connections to my beloved mom-in-law, Sis. All of this in a matter of minutes. The Universe answered when I asked!

Yes, I do believe in the Universe in action, and I believe that when we trust, when we are Aware...Receptive...Accepting...some amazing things happen and valuable information comes our way!

CHAPTER TWO

Off to Patagonia!

*"Follow your soul's calling and I will conspire with you for
success!" reminded the Universe.
"I am on my way!" answered an excited Me.*

My five-hour flight from Seattle to JFK International Airport in
New York was smooth. Long. Sometimes crossing the mass that is
the United States seems to take no time at all, other times I feel I
could be flying to Egypt. Today, it was brief and smooth, not a
bump in the sky. How odd. Turbulence over the Rocky
Mountains is the norm. Did I sleep through it? I don't remember
sleeping. Resting, head bobbing now and again, but not sleeping. I
wonder.

A blizzard in New York is forecast. The angst of weather issues
as we come into JFK, and an eight-hour layover, await before my
next flight. Buenos Aires and then on to El Calafate, Argentina in
the heart of Patagonia. I am *not* complaining. I am ecstatic to be

headed out on this next adventure but leery of landing during a snowstorm.

For all the air travel I have done in the last twenty years, one especially nasty flight from Seattle to Wenatchee, Washington on a small in-state hopper jet in 2005 has unsettled my nerves when it comes to turbulence. Ten years later, almost to the day as I think about it, and my palms sweat as I instinctively reach for the seat in front of me at the slightest bounce or bump.

It was the Friday of Super Bowl weekend and our hometown team, the Seattle Seahawks, was playing the Pittsburgh Steelers for the coveted title and rings. My Dad and stepmom, who live on the other side of the state from me—the dry and arid side of Washington State—were throwing a Super Bowl party. And, since I was long overdue for a visit, and driving the mountain passes of the Cascade mountains of Washington State in the winter was not a viable option, I opted for the quickie flight. Thirty-five minutes from Seattle to Wenatchee where Dad would meet me for a short one-hour drive to his home in Ephrata.

Super Bowl parties in the Pacific Northwest that weekend were met with a record windstorm, one that struck at its worst just as I was over the desolate Cascade Mountains in a twin-engine jet that sat about twenty anxious passengers. Seated in the front row, I had a crystal clear view of the flight attendant, strapped tight in her jumpseat. Her troubled face, 'Everything is okay; this is normal' smile glued in place did not fool me in the slightest. She was not okay, and if she was not okay…well, the fact that I felt the urge to lose my morning's breakfast would be considered quite normal.

If thirty-five minutes could last twenty-four hours, this flight did just that. Primarily a commuter flight taking busy executives and corporate salespeople home from a day in the state's largest city, I was among seasoned 'over the Cascades' flyers. Their faces said, "This is not okay." When we touched down, after a much jostled descent into the Columbia River Gorge, a cheer went up. Twenty people taking a deep collective breath and letting out a shout of joy! Twenty-one, actually, as our flight attendant was clapping right along with us. And, through the shaky laughter, I felt the tears begin to flow. Forty-eight years old, well-traveled, and crying like a baby as I exited the plane and walked straight into the arms of my father waiting at the gate.

That is why the thought of traveling into a blizzard as we reach New York had me fighting the urge to cry.

The blessing on this flight to New York's JFK airport is that, for whatever reason, I was not only upgraded first to Economy Comfort on this Delta flight—an extra five inches of up front legroom, a godsend for this six-foot, long-legged gal—I was then moved once again into First Class. The travel gods are watching out for me. I just kept wishing I was not on a red-eye so I might enjoy those first class cocktails!

As for the blizzard? We touched down under sun and scattered clouds. Not a snowflake in sight. Not a bump or a jostle. Glorious!

Here I sit in Terminal 7 at JFK waiting for Aerolíneas Argentinas to open their check in counters at 11:15 AM, three hours from now, so I can drop my backpack and go meandering in search of a meal. My Deuter pack, tucked into a backpack carry bag, is not the friendly travel companion it is when strapped on. When the padded waist belt and cushy shoulder straps are in place, it hugs my back; fits me perfectly. Tucked inside an oversized backpack travel bag, slung over my shoulder, it is weighty and awkward. This way, however, straps, clips, and the numerous talismans tied on the front do not threaten conveyor belts. Much easier although much heavier!

My bright orange, now well-marred, backpack was my trusted companion as I crossed northern Spain along the Camino Frances to Santiago de Compostela. Hefting it over my shoulders in the early morning dawn of Camino travel felt like coming home. Backpack and walking stick and I was complete.

After my return from the Camino in November, I found myself walking regularly to keep in shape for this trek I was now embarking on, but did so for two months without my pack. The day I loaded it, strapped it on, and set out on a local trail near home, boots tied tight and trekking poles clicking the pathway, I was in heaven.

How to even describe the utter sense of peace and joy as I buckled the straps, adjusted the hip band and set out fully loaded, if only for a practice walk. My soul was singing its song again... Camino song...melody playing through my heart and body.

One and a half miles down the trail and I bumped into my sister and her friend while they walked. The tears welled when expressing my joy at this walk today. Overwhelming emotion. Tears on the edges of my eyes pooled, ready to spill over. All I know is that I was feeling whole, happy, content. At complete peace.

Why did it feel so perfect to add the pack today? Mary suggested it was the final piece that spells "GO!" Is that it? Is it the pack that says, "YES, you are on your way, Kate. Walk with me and feel the freedom...hear the mud squish under your boots and see the colors around you... let my weight settle upon your shoulders and hips and prove we are off...I am the final piece that walks with you on your life adventure...I am a part of you."

And now, we are ready to explore again. This time the Patagonian Andes—the famed W Trek.

The meal pickings here at lower level Terminal 7 are slim to none. Upstairs, a myriad of check-in counters with no seating is clogged with early morning travelers. Any potential meal options, of which I trust there are many and quite varied, are found after security. So, for me, the lower level of 7 provides some seating, a small Subway sandwich outlet, and the perfunctory Starbucks, although a mini Starbucks sans sandwiches and salads. Thank goodness for that 6:00 AM First Class breakfast!

I am sharing a table for six with other waiting travelers while killing time, attempting to Facebook and email friends and family. The internet signal on my mini-iPad, my lightweight connection to the world when I am out on long distance walks, looks strong.

No connection. Walk over there...wander over here...no connection. So much for the complimentary internet offered in lower level Terminal 7. Certainly, I could hop to another network, one that undoubtedly would have me connected in a heartbeat, but paying for internet connection time in an airport goes against my grain. I find our American capitalist system of paying for everything in US airports frustrating and, quite frankly, embarrassing.

"WELCOME to the USA! We are so glad you are here to visit. A cart? You want a cart for your baggage? Well, whip out that credit card because you are about to be nailed with your first four-dollar airport charge Mr. and Mrs. Tourist!"

Years traveling in Europe and never did I pay for a cart.

"Internet. Yes, there is complimentary internet. It likely won't connect, but that's okay, for five dollars an hour you can buy time and have a signal that works. Just enter that credit card number.

What, you don't trust entering a credit card number while sitting in a busy international airport? Well, no internet for you then."

Yes, paying for internet is common in Europe too, but a free fifteen minutes is the norm. Enough to drop a line home letting your loved ones know you are safe, sound, and on your way to your next location. Civilized.

I am tired. Choosing to fall into negativity is not how I want to begin this adventure. I *know* better. I catch myself going into grumpy, bitchy mode and have to stop. It serves no purpose. I know this. It is not my normal state. I am not very proud of myself right now. Time to take a deep breath and focus on all that is right—all that makes my heart happy and grateful. Time to wander outside a bit and breathe some fresh air. That always helps!

And then, upstairs; check in and head to the next flight. Patagonia here I come!

CHAPTER THREE

Letting Go of Him, Again

"And what is it, Kate, you are so very afraid of?"
asked The Universe.
"Being rejected...not being loved," answered Me.

I have been in Argentina only a couple of days. But already I feel the aloneness settle in. These last months since returning from my Camino were filled with the joy of family, dear friends and holiday gatherings. I am living with my amazing sister Mary, who also happens to be my very dearest friend in the world, and her fifteen-year-old son, my nephew Cameron. Days are full which helps the time to fly by, helps the focus to remain *off* what I am missing and on the future.

But here I am, alone in southern Argentina, and the loss creeps back.

I am here to walk, however. These day hikes in the surrounding hills of El Chaltén will be practice for the much more difficult trail I will face in a few days when I reach Patagonian Chile and the famed W Trek. There I will spend six days tucked in the natural beauty of Torres del Paine National Park. It won't be a walk, it will be a hike, and for me that will be an undertaking. I have never truly hiked—hiked as in scrambling over river boulders, sliding down steep rocky pathways on my rear, and not trusting the footing under me. These four days in Argentina and El Chaltén are my warm-up.

The sun is shining. Eight AM and I am underway after a light breakfast and, as always, more cups of coffee than are truly healthy. Today I am headed across town and up the simple one hour hike to los Cóndores and las Aquilas. This hike takes me to a viewpoint overlooking the incredible panoramic views of the Adela, Torre, and Fitz Roy massifs. Photos of Fitz Roy, the snowcapped craggy edges so representative of the mountains of Patagonia, have piqued my interest since I was young. Patagonia has always held an allure. Never in my wildest dreams as a young girl could I have envisioned actually being here...surrounded by the beauty that is southern Argentina.

It has become my habit, since my Camino days, to watch for heart shaped rocks in the path. Amazing, when you keep a close eye out, they show themselves every few kilometers. Each one I cross is my moment to say a brief prayer of gratitude for someone in my life. I actually have deemed them *prayer rocks* and find my walks filled with more wonder when I focus on watching for these treasures and saying a 'thank-you.'

Crossing the bifurcation that will take me to las Aquilas viewpoint when I double back, a perfectly shaped heart rock lay at my feet. Stooping to pick it up, Jack's name crosses my mind, and I know this prayer of gratitude will be for him.

Within a few meters, I am at los Cóndores viewpoint, so-named as it is a natural viewpoint to catch Andean condors in their glide to and from the Rio Fitz Roy valley far below.

Prayer rock in hand, eyes focused on the magnificent scenery spilling forth before me, memories of another day watching elegant condor's sail in the winds bring forth a feeling of warmth.

I had crossed the great Pyrenees and was traveling down a steep rocky pathway from the heights into the valley below, home to Roncesvalles, the first Camino stop in northern Spain. Pairs of gigantic birds drifting high above on thermals caught my attention. Stunned at the grace and beauty of their flight, wingspans nearly six feet across, they soared with an elegance unfathomable for their size. No restrictions, no battling the winds...they instinctively knew when to surrender and float. They knew when to release and let the powers of the Universe treat them to joyful, easy flight.

It had been on that day, in those moments, that I chose to let go—chose to surrender to what was in my life and accept, once again, that I was exactly where I was meant to be. That Jack would no longer be in my world was a part of the plan. I could fight it, or I could accept the energies of the Universe and know that something grand was in store. My choice. Surrender...accept that my world had changed...or fight. I chose surrender and soar!

Excited voices bubble somewhere near. Amazed whispers bring me back to los Cóndores just as three pair of condor come into full view. At the trailhead an hour earlier, a chalkboard had shown that the last viewing had been very early yesterday morning; none reported since then. Today, blessed with sun and a light wind, they are back at play...soaring effortlessly between the heights of the hills and the steppe land below. Magnificent in their flight. Free. They instinctually know where to fly, when to release their powerful wings and simply soar. And I am witness. Cradling my prayer rock, my heart says a loving prayer of gratitude for the man who had been my husband and friend all these years. A man I love and always will. Blessed in this wondrous moment, I can send him love.

Doubling back a few meters, I take a left turn and head toward the viewpoint of las Aquilas...*the waters.* The path through fields of wildflowers leads me to a sweeping view of vast, inland, blue green Lago Viedma. Grand in size, from my outlook at the natural balcony viewpoint, it seems more an inland sea then a lake. Behind me, the massifs of Fitz Roy and the Adelas loom high overhead across the valley.

I am in awe!

Breathe...just breathe in this freedom. Breathe in and release all worries, all past, all hurts. Breathe in joy!

Breathe in gratitude.

It seems hard to comprehend that it has been almost a year since our marriage ended. April.

Last year in April is when the death knell word was spoken. Divorce. Divorce was the answer. Heartbroken, I knew in my deepest soul he was right. It had been coming for months...years perhaps...and there it was...divorce. Almost a year ago now.

So, where to settle my thoughts. Isn't it odd how one moment we can be overwhelmed with joy and the next we can find ourselves once again questioning. Anger...hurt...or gratitude. Gratitude. I choose gratitude. For all he gave, for all we were. Funny, the final climb above the Lago Viedma viewpoint gets easier. The air smells rich and settles warm on my shoulders. I refocus my thoughts.

Now and again, other day hikers pass by, stopping, stunned by the beauty of this isolated landscape ringed in snowcapped peaks. We smile at each other as we pass...my loneliness is gone. I offer them vibrations of love...they return the energy to me. A shift has occurred.

The remainder of my day is filled with camaraderie as I trek back in the company of a pair of Australian lovebirds adventuring in this faraway land. We stop in town for chilled cervezas and chat for an hour about travels. They seem astonished that a fifty-seven-year old woman is here alone on her way to hike the W trek. Their faces give them away. Am I crazy? Should I be here and choosing this hike in a few days' time?

No, I am here because this is exactly where I am meant to be. Smiling, I assure them that if I can walk five hundred miles across northern Spain I can handle fifty-seven miles of W Trek. Amazed at my Camino accomplishment, they agree!

A second cerveza downed and we are ready to part ways. Off they wander, hand in hand, reminding me how glorious love truly can be.

As I settle in for the night in a small local hotel I have booked for my days here at El Chaltén, the emotions of love and joy I felt throughout the day take hold. The emptiness turned grateful heart allow me to finally write the message to Jack that has been composing itself for the last months. The message I want him to know as we move forward, each on our own paths.

Dear Jack,

If the world were to end tomorrow, I would want you to know how truly grateful I am for the wonderful years we have shared.

I am grateful for experiences and adventures with you, which opened my eyes to this amazing world. I am grateful for the love and generosity you showed as a step-dad to our Greg. I am grateful for the treasure of having your Mom with us in her last months.

I am grateful for your humor...making me laugh year after year. I am grateful for moments you were able to help me see myself in my family dynamics more clearly. I am grateful for pats on the bottom, morning hugs, and "hi baby" in the morning when I woke you.

I am grateful for your love of our doggie children and the fun in having them in our lives. I am grateful for the parties we cohosted and the friends we had over the years...the fun...the music...the laughter.

No matter what you may want to believe at times, I wish you only the best and focus on only the best. There is much to be thankful for in these last years. You are a blessing to me and will always be a blessing to me.

This message has been on my mind for several weeks...it is time to send it your way.

With love always,

Kate

I read and reread my words, searching for any hidden meaning he may find, wanting only the love and compassion I feel for this man to show. In the end, I take a deep breath, bless my words with love and push 'send.'

And now to sleep!

CHAPTER FOUR

El Chaltén—
Oh How I Love to Sing!

"And if you choose to sing? asked the Universe.
"I am alive!" answered Me.

So strange how when alone, away from everyone and everything familiar, the mind can bounce between ecstatic highs, elated excitement of what is to come, to almost depressed lows. My heart feels overjoyed at where I am and what lies ahead, both on this trip as well as life in general and then empties in a flash.

When the day started, I could hardly force myself out of bed. Partially physically tired from the extensive travel, partially emotionally worn, I just felt *off.*

But, I am *not* here to lay around, so a swift kick in my own hind-end, a long, hot shower, plenty of rich Argentinian coffee and off! There are amazing sites in the mysterious land.

And, what a glorious day! A short nine-kilometer circuit took me to enchanting Laguna Capri with its breathtaking views from Mirador Fitz Roy.

This morning, Mount Fitz Roy, partially hidden in fast moving clouds, was not the clear photo opportunity I had hoped to find. Nonetheless, I sat mesmerized watching clouds shift, veils of a dancer offering a subtle glimpse every so often.

Laguna Capri is a favorite day hike for those trekking the countless trails of this Argentinian wonderland. Depths of blue, tones rich and deep beyond description fade one into another as the waters shift in the breeze.

As hikers approach to take in the view, I am keenly aware I have nabbed the perfect picnic locale. My spot on the edge of the lake, full vista spread before me, is the photo opportunity for which everyone vies. Shall I move? Is it fair? I stretch my legs; settle in to soak in the sun.

A short two kilometers beyond my envied lunch view, I take a short climb to reach Mirador Fitz Roy. Earlier clouds have scattered and Fitz Roy, 3,480 meters in height, stands majestically over Laguna Capri, a watchful eye over the lands below.

Mount Fitz Roy—the original name is Chaltén, which means "smoking mountain." This is due to a rare aeolic phenomenon, with the top surrounded by clouds, giving the mountain a smoking volcano look.

In 1877, an expedition led by Perito Moreno baptized it Fitz Roy, in memory of the sailor that explored the channels in Tierra del Fuego and the Santa Cruz River during the Charles Darwin expedition. And, at this moment in time, I am given witness to one of the most incredible sights in Patagonia Argentina.

Awestruck, I am filled with an overwhelming sense of gratitude for such a blessing. Settling onto a smoothed boulder seat to bear witness, the concept of time becomes non-existent as I find myself fully engaged with the glory of nature surrounding me. Twittering birds rustle leaves on the trees as they light. Azure waters of the lagoon lap the pebbles on the beach...swish...swish. Breezes blowing ever so lightly catch a bough above my head...creeeak...almost imperceptible. I am completely connected to the earth and sky. The energies of this sacred land buzz through me, my very being amplified as I sit one with the Universe.

Voices, laughing, break the silence; sever the serenity as they approach the mirador. A last glimpse skyward, for now, as I stand to gather daypack and trekking poles. A glance at my watch confirms it is time to head back toward town and on to Chorrillo del Salto, an easy seven kilometer circuit once I reach the base of today's' earlier climb.

Chorrillo del Salto, direct translation 'trickle jump' which I reach at about 4:00 PM, looks crowded with other walkers. An easy hike, most here have wandered the final kilometer to the falls from a carpark just off the gravel one-lane road. Part of the local national park system, this hike is renowned and draws many on this sunny summer February day.

Rounding a final bend, the hidden twenty-foot falls spill before me into a shallow transparent pool. Water's sparkle so clear each underlying pebble can be counted, each earth tone glistening in the late afternoon sun. And silence. At least fifty others are settled on rocks at the perimeter and below the falls. Voices are nonexistent. Faces gaze in wonder at the beauty surrounding us, tilted toward a warm embracing sun. Water crashing to the pool below is the only sound and it is heavenly.

I step gingerly over boulders in the pool, claiming an empty rock directly facing this magnificent sight. Sun beating on my shoulders, off come my boots and socks. Toes free to test the water temperature. Once hot, feet now cooled. Glorious. A brief look around and I see others dangling legs, up to their knees, in the refreshing waters. Sandwiches and snacks are being munched, water guzzled in the late afternoon heat. I too take advantage of another of Patagonia's magical locales, cooling my Nestea bottle in these mountain waters before taking that first awaited sip. Life does not get better! Here is heaven.

An hour later and it is time to wander back to my hotel, drop off pack and poles and find a bite to eat for the evening. El Chaltén is a busy place. February is the height of the summer trekking season and El Chaltén is Argentina's premier trekking locale. Limited supplies in the local grocery stores speak to columns of hikers heading into the mountains for this four-day holiday weekend. Shelves are bare of basic food supplies.

Three mini-mercados later, I manage to track down a small bag of nuts, my trail protein for the next day. A block from my hotel sits the taproom/restaurant my hotel staff suggested for a bite to eat and camaraderie with fellow walkers/hikers. La Cerveceria offers indoor air-conditioned seating and the loveliest backyard outdoor dining area. Tables are busy with hikers enjoying an end of the day local brew and tapas. Grabbing a small table near the edge of the lawn, I settle in. Pack, poles, and boots lay beside me on the grass. My toes stretch to welcome the cool breeze. Looking around, I notice most everyone else has the same idea. Here is the greatest benefit to sitting outdoors!

The beer is cold, refreshingly cold. My server, a young lady with dreadlocks piled atop her head, recommends the specialty of the house for a light bite. Empanadas, the traditional stuffed pastry found in many Latin countries. An order will give me four pieces. "Plenty!" she advises.

From somewhere near the corner door leading to the interior, music floats in the late afternoon air. Welcomed beer in hand, I wander toward the folksy tunes and find a solo guitarist perched on a barstool. Slicked back ebony, shoulder-length hair and deep brown eyes, he smiles when he catches my gaze, encouraging me to sing along. The clientele is a mix of Argentines enjoying their long weekend holiday and the international set: South Americans, Europeans, and North Americans who have gathered in El Chaltén.

The mood is light, laughter and easy chatter, some singing along to what sounds like a traditional and well-known local folk song. Not knowing the words, I smile back and give him a "I don't know the words" signal with my hands and a shake of my head. As the song ends, an appreciative applause breaks out from the crowd. Obviously more of them know this favorite! A quick check over my shoulder tells me my food has not yet arrived so I stay where I am, waiting for his next number.

"All my bags are packed, I'm ready to go. I'm standing here outside your door. I hate to wake you up to say good-bye...Leavin' on a jet plane...."

Everyone seems to know the chorus and the entire outdoor seating area erupts in song. "...Don't know when I'll be back again...."

I am in my element, joining the crowd in a strong happy voice. Of all the sixty's folk songs he could have chosen, Mr. Argentinian guitarist chooses one that brings me back to happy memories of singing. I so love to sing! I have always loved to sing; I am alive when I sing!

This closet is magnificent! A true walk-in closet in my bedroom! Of course, I share this room with my sisters Annie and Jeannie, but that's okay. We are finally in a real house. The housing projects are back in Clarkston and we now live in a town with snow-covered mountains on one side and the Strait of Juan de Fuca on the other. Incredible! I never knew there was such a place.

When we drove the U-Haul with everything we owned, which really was not a lot, from Clarkston to Port Angeles, my first glimpse of the waters of south Puget Sound was breathtaking. We were at the ocean as far as I was concerned. That trip, the drive to a new life, brought us here to this rented house on Seventh Street. A 'real house' with a yard, and a porch. A 'real house' with big bedrooms (ours easily slept the three of us in our twin size beds). And, a walk-in closet—a grand walk-in closet!

I'm sure if I saw it now I would giggle, but at the time, it seemed immense. Of course, it was not really a walk-in closet. No, this was a nightclub where my gorgeous, talented, svelte Barbie was star of the show! My songstress Barbie was a redhead, which made her all the more dear to my strawberry-blonde eleven-year-old self. And SHE could sing! She sang Mary Hopkins, Bobby Sherman, Dionne Warwick...if it was a hit in 1968, she sang it!

'California Dreamin' was her best number; it was Mamas and the Papas hip. Barbie knew all the words perfectly. She was simply groovy on this song!

Redheaded Barbie's dedicated audience, my sister Annie, and her entourage of Barbies and Chrissy dolls, paid homage to my Barbie's outstanding talents. They were a small, but highly appreciative, group who came to listen to Lounge Singer Barbie's matinee performances on Saturday and Sunday afternoons. During the school week she might get in a show after homework was done. The weekends were her best time...the time of week she put on her greatest performances.

Working her shoebox stage, Barbie was striking in open-toed royal blue heels tucked under the full white satin skirt of her nightclub gown. She was a star, just stepped out of an MGM musical movie set. Tight blue shimmering bodice, waist cinched, her glittered skirt flowed around her as she twirled and danced.

And not only did she look stunning, that girl could sing! She heard her audience go wild as she belted lyric after lyric:

"Do you know the wayyyyyy to San Jose? I'm going back someday, I'm afraid I'll lose my way..." Clap, clap, clap!

"THOOOOOOOSSE were the DAAAAYYSSS my friend, we thought they'd never end, we'd sing and dance..."

Cheering from the crowd...CLAP...CLAP...CLAP! Yeaaa!

Stealthily, Annie was on her knees, audience gathered in her arms, as she scooted quickly to the door.

"NO! Don't leave...I have an encore!"

away sending him only love, recognizing that his rejection, his hurtful words, are not of me. It is what he cannot face in himself. He cuts off those he has loved because he cannot face the man he has become. He hides—in solitude, in booze, in addictive behaviors—he hides from life and love.

Jack will be my greatest lesson in unconditional love. No matter what happens in the future, I will love him and wish him peace. And in doing so I learn my lessons: not to be afraid, not to rely on what someone else feels toward me in finding my happiness. I am whole in my own right. I am in no need of someone else's acceptance. I am strong and capable.

And so I ask myself why this email from him now? Why this message on Valentine's Day of all days? And why, what synchronicity is at play, that one more time I am at the 'ends of the earth' as I let him go...again.

Funny, these last few days hiking El Chaltén I have been aware of him; aware of us. And now this letter and everything is so much easier. Well, perhaps easier is the wrong word. Perhaps "makes it so much more obvious" is a better phrase. Yes, his words make it obvious.

It is as though I am walking him out of my system. Walking until I feel cleansed and ready for something new. This trek is indeed a part of my Camino of the Soul...a heart trek. At the end of my walk in Spain, gazing at the Atlantic on the cliffs of Finisterre, I thought the past had been released. Not so.

Mourning, releasing, is a process. Cleansing, clearing...starting over again, and again and again...day after day...a new beginning and a new belief that I will be happy and well again. That I will be loved again. I recognize I am walking to empty my heart and head of all that aches; all that feels empty. Filling it instead with air and nature. Filling it with the sights and sounds of a world I never before looked to discover, a world that has always been at my doorstep and now feels the very core of me.

And I am very truly grateful to him for having brought me here, through his rejection, to find what I was meant to be. The journey is underway. The final *how* is not yet known, but I trust I am on the right path. I know in the depths of my soul that I am following a track I am meant to follow.

This last chapter of my life is a lesson in trust. Trusting in the soul knowledge that *nothing in my life is out of order.* I am exactly where I am meant to be. My job is to trust. Intend, and believe the rest will come. And it will...it already has. That I can send a letter of love and gratitude, and accept his response of rejection with love and compassion, validates that love has taken over...that gratitude is my path.

And this morning I feel content. I am able to write these words of love, and they flow freely from my heart confirming I have taken a mighty step in my soul trek.

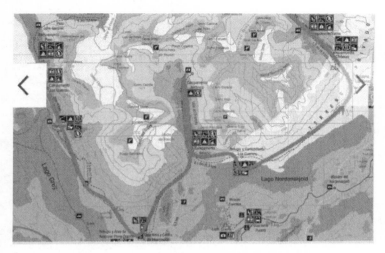

W Trek, Torres del Paine

My Camino Prayer

Because I believe the Universe conspires on our behalf...because I believe angels are actively involved in our daily life and offer amazing insight if we listen and watch...because I believe in the beauty of each day and know we have the opportunity to choose our thoughts and state of mind...I see this glorious day begin to unfold and know in my soul these travels will be safe, inspiring, a chance once again, to behold the magnificence of this planet we call home...and I feel blessed.

CHAPTER SIX

Welcome to Torres del Paine

"And are you ready for this? asked the Universe.
"I am!" answered a confident Me.

Torres del Paine—Towers of Blue— in the tongue of the Tehuelche Indians, native people to this corner of the globe.

Granite, sawtoothed peaks split the skies, slicing the clouds in their climb. The first view of los Torres del Paine, across the turquoise waters of Lago Amarga, was breathtaking. Every camera, every iPad, clicked as selfies, group shots, 'please, will you take my photo?' memories were collected.

Yet, what a barren place. After a six-hour ride on a less than modern forty-four passenger tour bus, the drive from El Chaltén, Argentina to the parkland of Torres del Paine across the border into southern Chile, I almost wondered if I should stay. Dry, gritty dirt whipped the bus windows coming at us in sixty kilometer per hour gusts. Has this whole W Trek idea been a horrid mistake?

On the bus, the chatter is about conditions, just like these, all week. Approximately half the group of thirty-three are here to hike over the next days. The others are on a very, very long day trip just to view these magnificent young peaks. Twelve million years old, the peaks of southern Argentina and Chile in the Andes are considered some of the youngest on earth! It boggles my mind.

I am totally prepared and ready for some inclement weather, but frankly, hiking a week in these winds is not my idea of fun or purposeful. The land is desolate. Toughened by lack of rain, the steppe land we rattle through is wind-blown, colorless. Except for the lakes: majestic, gemstonecolored seas set into monochromatic landscape.

Guanaco, a native llama-esque creature, graze on dried brush near the road. Families of six, eight, and ten gather, noshing on prickly calafate bushes. Wild on the steppe and throughout Patagonia, here they pay no mind as we rattle past kicking up dust storms in our wake. Each sighting brings a cry from someone on the bus,

"Look! Guanaco. Slow, slow, please," and the camera's pop. Cruising at sixty kilometers per hour, ninety-five percent of our sightings today have gone undocumented, I am sure.

Gigantic hawks balance on wooden fence posts marking the boundaries of the park. Focused, they patiently wait for a mid-day snack to scamper into view. Jack rabbits dart across the fields. And ostrich. No. Franco our guide has just pointed them out and calls them rhea, a relative of the ostrich and emu. An endangered species native to southern South America, they roam wild in the steppe.

As far as I am concerned they are ostrich!

I'm not quite sure why I am so intrigued. Bouncing, round feathered bodies perched atop gangly knobby-kneed legs. Their gait odd; none too graceful. An awkward teenage girl teetering atop her first pair of high heels. Unstable...self-aware.

When was it? I think I was probably fourteen years old. Yes, junior high school. Dressed in the maroon colors of our junior high football team, our choir jumpsuits were all the rage. One-piece zip-up–the-front jumpsuits—perfectly suited for the 5'11" me. Add my first heels and I stood a head above the other girls. Hell, I stood a head above the boys!

My first high heels. Black, open toed sandal style heels. I loved them! Worn to impress. This was the concert where I sang a solo knowing that the high school music instructor, Mr. Grier, was in the audience, watching and considering several of us as potential members of the elite high school swing vocal group, Pops Choir. This was the night! If he liked what he heard I would be called in for an audition and if that went well, next year I would join the ranks of high school vocalists I so admired.

Could he see me wobble? Were they all laughing at my skinny frame, not yet the curves I would develop in the next couple of years. I walked gingerly to the center of the gymnasium floor where the microphone stood waiting. Guitar in hand, my song of choice was Peter, Paul and Mary's 'Leavin' on a Jet Plane.' Folksy, the perfect key, and one I could belt! My long skinny, knobby-kneed legs shook beneath the jumpsuit pant legs. Thank God they are hidden!

"Straight back Kathy, walk straight and tall." I could hear my Mom's voice in my ears. I felt my ankles fighting to stay steady...damn high heels...why did I wear them tonight? Clumsy me, still one to round corners too quickly and catch a baby toe on the doorframe.

Tall, gawky, strawberry blonde hair and unfashionable glasses, I was not yet grown into myself...an ostrich in a maroon jumpsuit meandering across the junior high school gymnasium floor on two-inch heels.

"...and now take a look...look out to your left...it's a bit misty, but you can just see the los Torres. Look everyone!" Franco's voice boomed into the quite unnecessary mic.

"We will stop the bus here for photos. Lago Amarga and los Torres. And, watch the sky.

We often see Andean condor here at the lago shore. If you see them let everyone else know! Okay, back to the bus in ten minutes please."

Once again, I am blessed with the magnificent condor. Four glorious creatures soaring high overhead. At their height, it seems they are dodging cotton ball clouds high above. These condor, however, are working against the howling winds. Thermals for drifting, soaring with no care, are not today's conditions. Still, in the magnificence of their flight they lift my heart, remind me that I can choose to soar!

Throughout the remainder of the day tour, we venture in a large loop encircling Lagos Amarga and Nordenskjold. Glacial lakes, depths of color I have never before seen in such an arid environment.

Coming from the Pacific Northwest, I am quite used to glorious ice blue glacial lakes tucked behind the curve of a pine tree lined highway...hidden surprises Mother Nature has devised just to take our breath away. Day trips into the Cascade Mountains, the home of spectacular Mount Rainier, offer a myriad of hikes to magical hidden lakeshores. Even across the Cascades into eastern Washington State, deep gorges, cut through the harsh earth millions of years ago during the last Ice Age, are home to lakes incredible in size and color. But none, none that match what I see in front of me. Lago Amarga, sea foam green, small waterspouts forming as the Patagonian winds whip.

Back on the bus to our next stop in twenty minutes. A short walk and we stand on a rocky precipice overlooking rippling waterfalls as one lake cascades into the next. Emerald pools sparkle below as rainbows glisten in the mist. With winds howling to gusts of one hundred kilometers per hour, we crouch low to the ground, hats and glasses no longer perched atop our heads Franco, a long-time guide in this area, alerts us in his booming voice:

"DO NOT stand arms outstretched along the edges. Yes, I know, it makes a wonderful photo. You can be blown right into the rocks below! It happened last week! She was a small woman, she did not listen and was knocked into the lake. DO NOT stand on the edges...please!"

I believe him. If I am being buffeted to the point of walking in a crouched position to glimpse a better view over the edge, I can only imagine one of the shorter, lighter women in our group.

Again, I find myself doubting why I am here and if I should stay or skip the W entirely; ride the bus back to Argentina with the day-trippers. Decision time!

* * * *

Pisco sour balanced on the arm of an Adirondack-style chair, I sit here in the warmth of the sun on the grassy lawn of Torres del Paine Refugio. I am quite at peace with my decision to stay and continue with my hike as planned.

As I left the tour bus behind, a smaller shuttle awaited. This shuttle took only thirty minutes to reach the hostel where I am spending my first night. Within a fifteen-minute ride, we were entering the park proper. The barren dry dirt of the steppe was left behind as quickly as one pulls the velvet curtain at the end of a stage play.

New scene: colorful purple calafate bushes and trees in varying shades of green. A microclimate allowing Mother Earth to toss a bit of color on her shoulders.

Others are gathering outside, having found their bunks and done a cleanup from the dusty day. Dinner is in an hour for the first sitting. I have a two-hour wait until I dine. Sitting number two is my schedule; I was told as I checked in and was shown to my bunk.

Sipping my complimentary pisco sour, journal in hand, I am quite content to watch the comings and goings of arriving hikers as I document the day. First: pisco sour - How divine! It is a delicious taste treat. Chilean brandy liqueur from distilled grapes is mixed with lemon juice, sugar, an egg white and then given a martini-style shake. Delightful!

How do I feel now? Now that I know I will stay and hike the W Trek? Excited. No nerves, simply the anticipation of what the next days will hold as I venture into this awaited trek. Journaling my thoughts as I bask in this magnificent setting allows focus.

Questions: what do I truly wish to create for myself? Will I form a company offering walks to other women my age, women who crave the adventure, but are not quite ready to take it on alone? Will my writing flow? This trip needs to be documented. Will I take the time each day to capture emotions, new understandings...the landscape? The landscape must come home with me in words.

And, will the magical communications with my sister Jeannie, Sis, my mom-in-law, and MJ reach me here? That's a silly statement. Energy...it is all a matter of energy. They can touch my soul anywhere; anywhere because they are everywhere with their angel energy. No here or there...then or now. Energy flowing. Transmitting love from one plane to the next. It is in the walking that my heart and soul are most open to receive their wisdom from new realms. They will be here!

Smiling as I write this, I know I am safe. Watched over...guided. I am exactly where I am meant to be. All I have to do is listen...listen to the whispers.

What awaits?

CHAPTER SEVEN

Christmas Eve

"When your heart takes you home, Kate, what do you see?"
asked the Universe.
"I see Christmas," answered Me.

It dawned on me as I walked along the elevated ridge above the valley cut that leads to El Chileno on this first day, that the tap, tap of my walking sticks lulls me to daydream. Aware of my surrounding on some level, caught in a trance of childhood memories on another. Click...click...click...tumblers opening compact compartments of joyous memories.

Perched on a rock overlooking the lago below, I adjust my boots and socks. Perhaps I should just take them off and let the toes breathe for while...let the breeze caress hot, tired feet. Never having been a long-distance walker or hiker for that matter, the valuable lesson of 'loosen your boots; take them off if you can' sunk in quickly on the Camino. Boots and socks...off they come.

47

My feet are crying for air; here is the perfect spot. A break, some water, air the socks.

Dangling from my trekking poles, they lift in the breeze...perpendicular to the ground below. It is eerily quiet; no other hikers near. Only the sound of the wind through the canyon. I feel myself drifting...head nodding ever so slightly. My socks on my poles flutter....

Each Christmas Eve, the socks were brought out and laid neatly across the back of the couch. There are no fireplaces in the housing projects of Clarkston, WA. The couch works! Six socks, gifts from Grandma and Grandpa.

Red Christmas socks with white cuffs wrapped in a sparkly gold braid. Each sock emblemmed with a white angel. Each sock adorned with our name. I am a Kathy, mine sits next to Mom's as I am the oldest.

Mom, Kathy, Anne, Jeanne, Joel and Mary...that's us. In the morning, they will be filled with treats and small gifts—practical gifts for the most part—precious all the same. There will be an orange tucked in the toe for filling, helping it to perch on the couch cushions. And a banana will stick out of the top. Part of traditional Christmas morning breakfast before church: ooey gooey cinnamon rolls, an orange and a banana. That the fruits are truly a practical sock-filling device does not matter. They help make for a FULL Christmas stocking in a child's eye. The goal: make it look plentiful! We are kids; it is about the show! More importantly, it is about the tradition and Christmas socks, and how they are packaged has to be consistent. Tradition. Creatures of habit, children. Memories being created.

The socks will be positioned so they overflow. So full, a color book or paper doll set has to be sitting underneath as it simply will not fit. So much! Each item is wrapped. Wrapped and ribboned in paper that has not been seen this season. Santa paper...North Pole paper! The magic! But that's for tomorrow morning.

6:50 Christmas Eve...time to open a gift. Tradition is one gift at 7:00 PM. One gift only. We get to choose from those already under the tree. Gifts from grandparents, our Dad, perhaps something from aunts and uncles. Mom has tucked something under for each of us as well. A small gift especially from her. Oh the dilemma of choosing just the perfect gift. Still two hours until bedtime. I so hope I don't pick pajamas! I want a record, or a book. Perhaps a game...something to do as this long evening progresses.

Five little children (I am only ten years old) on their tummies, under the tree as far as possible without touching...no touching the packages! That is a rule. We can look...we cannot touch! Which one shall I choose?

"Okay kids! It is seven o'clock. You can choose one present to open! Do you know which one? No shaking packages...I think you all have checked those tags and know which ones are yours?" She is so correct about that! We have been on our bellies, noses to packages, for the last week peeking at tags...sneaking a touch here and there. Shhh, don't tell Mom!

"Who wants to go first?"

We take turns, one by one, opening a gift. Never all at once. One by one draws the excitement out...allows time to slow as tags are read, ribbons pulled off and packages ripped into. One by one. With five of us, it takes at least thirty minutes. Thirty minutes closer to bed. Thirty minutes closer to Santa! Well, of course I no longer believe. But the others do! I am in on this oh so special secret and she has taught me how to help make it fun...she has taught me the tricks of being her elf and helping.

8:00 PM. Gathered in our jammies (some new if that was the chosen gift); we sit next to her and at her feet. It is time for the Christmas stories. First the Bible story. She reads from the family Bible.

> *"And it came to pass in those days, that there went out a decree from Caesar Augustus that all the world should be taxed.*
>
> *(And this taxing was first made when Cyrenius was governor of Syria.) And all went to be taxed, every one into his own city.*
>
> *And Joseph also went up from Galilee, out of the city of Nazareth, into Judaea, unto the city of David, which is called Bethlehem (because he was of the house and lineage of David)*
>
> *To be taxed with Mary his espoused wife, being great with child.*
>
> *And so it was, that, while they were there, the days were accomplished that she should be delivered.*

And she brought forth her firstborn son, and wrapped him in swaddling clothes, and laid him in a manger; because there was no room for them in the inn.

And there were in the same country shepherds abiding in the field, keeping watch over their flock by night.

And, lo, the angel of the Lord came upon them, and the glory of the Lord shone round about them: and they were sore afraid.

And the angel said unto them, Fear not: for, behold, I bring you good tidings of great joy, which shall be to all people.

For unto you is born this day in the city of David a Saviour, which is Christ the Lord. And this shall be a sign unto you; Ye shall find the babe wrapped in swaddling clothes, lying in a manger.

And suddenly there was with the angel a multitude of the heavenly host praising God, and saying,

Glory to God in the highest, and on earth peace, good will toward men."

~ Luke 2, 1-14, King James Version (KJV)

Closing the Bible with reverence, she takes a deep breath.

"There, now it is time to put baby Jesus in the manger," is her next announcement. Of course, we already know this happens next; this is tradition. It is how we do Christmas Eve. It can and will never change. It just is!

Our manger scene has been with us since before I was born. There is a three-sided brown toned stable with moss growing on the sides. The figurines of Joseph and Mary are surrounded by the three wise men, a shepherd with his one sheep and two cows. A glittering angel floats overhead guarding this sacred scene. Everyone is in place. They have been since our home was decorated shortly after Thanksgiving. Now, because it is finally Christmas Eve, baby Jesus is placed gently between Joseph and Mary. Our baby Jesus is already in his manger bed. Our tradition: the youngest child places baby Jesus. Since our sister Mary is still so little, only just two years old Joel will receive the honor. Four years old, on his tippy toes, he reaches to the bookshelf, which has been home to the manger scene all season. Baby Jesus is in place.

Little children.

"Does anyone need to go potty? This is the time!" Annie and I scamper down the hallway in a race for the bathroom. Jeannie and Joel anxiously await our return as Mom checks toddler Mary for dry pants.

She is making sure we are all ready for the second phase of the Christmas story readings, the BEST part. Everyone back in their places as she opens our favorite Christmas storybook.

"T'was the night before Christmas and All through the house, not a creature was stirring, not EVEN a mouse! The stockings were hung by the chimney with care, in hopes that St. Nicholas soon would be there. The children were nestled...."

Every sentence comes to life; each character's voice unique, full and rich. She is a master storyteller. We sit in rapt attention. Time stands still.

"...and they hear him exclaim as he drove out of sight MERRY CHRISTMAS TO ALL AND TO ALL A GOOD NIGHT!"

Five little children in chorus, "THE END!"

It is almost bedtime. Yawns are beginning. We have waited and waited for this night. Christmas music, favorite sing-along holiday songs, has played since the day after Thanksgiving. NEVER until Friday after Thanksgiving. Then "Little Drummer Boy" my favorite, spins over and over on our old record player. Christmas music has played, the tree has been decorated with precious handmade treasures and tinsel. And strings of popcorn! We have created paper cut out snowflakes on Saturday afternoons to adorn the windows. We have baked traditional treats.

Mexican wedding cake cookies, holiday sugar cookies cut in the shapes of stars and bells. There have been peanut butter cookies, jam thumbprints, and gingerbread cookies.

This afternoon, final letters to Santa were written. Earlier today, Christmas candy bowls were pulled from the back of a cupboard, washed and dried with care, and placed on end tables near the couch. In the morning when I lift the lid, the milky white

Christmas candy bowl will be filled with brightly colored ribbon candy. A deep green dish on a pedestal will hold M&M's. It happens every year. It is Christmas. This is tradition!

And now, time for the final magic. Stockings are placed. One, two, three, four, five and six. Stories are read. We have all stood in a ring in the kitchen watching as Mom pours a glass of milk and places the cookie plate on the table.

A small cereal bowl is placed next to Santa's cookie plate. Two cookies for Santa and Cheerios for the Reindeer. Reindeer love Cheerios! They eat them every year. Everyone else leaves carrots. We leave Cheerios!

Just outside the front door, the bowl of Cheerios is left to be gobbled up by hungry working reindeer. Santa's cookies and milk sit on the coffee table. Homemade holiday sugar cookies that we have all helped to decorate. The best!

One last thing to do. And this is so, so important. Two reddish orange decorative birds, tiny finches, are tucked on the tree with the other ornaments. We need to make sure we know where they are placed. Mentally we make note which side of the tree and the branches they are on. These birds are magic! At the midnight hour, as Christmas Eve becomes Christmas Day, they fly! Two little plastic finch birdies flit from one branch to the next, finally settling on a resting place for the remainder of the season. In the morning, we will hunt to find them because they WILL have flown. They always do! They are magic. Christmas is magic! Mom is magic...gifted, creative, loving, exhausted...magic.

"...Hey, are these yours? We found these socks just over there. They must have blown away while you had your eyes closed. Here you go! Buenas días!"

My hiking socks are handed back as two young trekkers move on their way, their poles tapping...click...click...click...the tumblers spin. The doors click shut. For now.

CHAPTER EIGHT

Refugio Chileno—Lunch Ballet

"Do you see the magic in the dance?" asked the Universe.
"I see it in others, I am not sure I see it in me,"
answered an intrigued Me.

Peeking through the cut-out from dining hall to the kitchen, I watch the ballet in action. Preparing the *'to go'* lunches is a carefully choreographed dance in a tightly packed service kitchen. A hearty breakfast of buttered, toasted bread, thick heavy bread, and an egg and sausage casserole has been served and cleared away at Refugio Chileno. Hikers are gathering their gear for the day, while stretching to loosen tight muscles before the day's endeavors. Outside on the patio, boots left from the night before, airing in the cool mountain breeze, are laced snug and tight on feet ready to hit the trail.

An eerie mist envelops the refugio grounds; the swinging bridge we crossed yesterday now lost from view.

My backpack is parked against the rail on the patio just outside the main doors. One of at least forty, perhaps more, waiting to be hoisted onto shoulders, buckles snapped tight. All mine needs before the final tie down is today's lunch sack. Several of us sip a last cup of rich South American coffee as we watch the ongoing performance in the kitchen.

Ciabatta rolls, sliced and stacked become playing cards dealt quickly onto the counter: ten wide, three deep. Bottom...top...bottom...top. Slap...slap...a spatula of dark mustard crosses the first bun and every second bun in turn. Bottom halves ready for the next layer. Lettuce, romaine by the looks, takes its place on the bun. Next a slice of cheese—no, two slices of local white cheddar—are stacked on the lettuce bed.

Finally, a thick slice of baked ham. Ensemble complete. Dancer number one, having created his masterpiece, flops the top bun on each and quickly passes them off to the aluminum foil lady...Dancer number two. A twenty-something beauty, dark curly hair pulled tightly from her face, she begins her solo.

Center the sandwich and fold the foil: one side, two, three, four. Snug, so no air leaks through. Her hands fly across the tin foil as she maneuvers to keep the pace as sandwiches fly her direction.

Brown paper bags, dancing in the breeze from a tiny kitchen window, sit open on the back prep counter. Slightly larger than the lunch sacks I remember from grade school, smaller than a grocery store bag, they stand at attention ready to do their part.

Dancer number three, a tall, lanky, outdoorsy type, tucks a juice box and a piece of fruit into the bag, creating a solid base at the bottom of the sack—easier to pack this way. He tosses in a protein bar and a granola snack bar, snuggles in a twelve-ounce water bottle and adds the entree: the well-wrapped, perfectly crafted, assembly line 'get these folks out the door, the next group will be here in three hours' sandwich. No folding the top of the bag...yet. Today there is an extra treat.

Dancer number four sashays down the hall and into the work area carrying a basket.

"Un momento!" she shouts as she rounds the corner.

"Tenemos galletas. Anadir una galleta." We have cookies; add a cookie, she shouts at number three.

Individually wrapped homemade cookies are positioned at the top of each bag; easy to reach for the mid-morning break. Whaa la! Two more rounds of the same dance and forty-five bags are ready for delivery!

* * * *

My hike today will take me from Refugio Chileno where I spent the night, back down the ridge trail I climbed yesterday, and on to los Cuernos, the Horns.

I know from listening to the chatter during dinner that this sector of the trek is considered the most majestic. Los Cuernos, '*the horns*' in Spanish, rise more than eight thousand feet straight up above Lago Nordenskjold. Others at the shelter last night, having walked the W Trek in reverse, called it their best walking day yet.

As I grab a lunch bag and tuck it safely in my pack, careful not to squish what will be a well-earned meal later today, my spirit is light...excited about the day ahead. It is a long walk...one of the longer of the five days, but that doesn't cause concern. After all, I walked twelve to fourteen miles a day for thirty-seven days last year on el Camino. No problem! Confidence oozing, I set off to discover what Day Two on the trail will bring!

Yesterday upon reaching Refugio Chileno I, like most others, left our larger packs and swapped into small day packs. Large enough for the essentials: water, a fleece, and a rain jacket, the daypack would be more than enough to trek toward the renowned base of los Torres del Paine. Two days ago I saw these incredible peaks from across Lago Amarga. The second half of yesterday took me through forested glades, high above the river running below. Birds twittered as the rush of the water echoed up the hillside.

The hike to the base of los Torres, a viewpoint famed worldwide, was to take only three to four hours round trip. The afternoon air, although laced with short spouts of drizzle, was warm enough to hike sans a fleece or jacket. My long-sleeved, orange, dri-wick tee was just enough over a short-sleeved tee underneath.

The trekking poles my son, Gregory and daughter-in-law, Allie, had given me as Christmas gift upon my return from the Camino, had certainly earned their keep as the forest disappeared and the true hike up to los Torres base began.

The path followed a mountain creek bed. No problem. I simply had to watch footing carefully in crisscrossing the creek, attempting to keep my boots dry in the few places water pooled. In a matter of minutes, the angle of the path jumped from a simple climb to steep corners. Accurate pole placement essential as I pulled myself forward.

Los Torres base, about a kilometer and a half ahead by my calculations, was tucked somewhere across the field of lava rock I now saw before me. Centuries old volcanic eruptions created this wonder of nature. The peaks loomed overhead, beckoning me to take a deep breath and continue up along the narrow winding path cutting its way through the moonscape rock fields.

Stopping to take in the incredible view and contemplate where I, Kate Elliott, nonhiker woman, was standing, it occurred to me that the view to the Paine massif, encircling the valley, was becoming obscured. Misty fog, not heavy by any means, but enough to erase the scene to some degree, was rolling in. One and a half kilometers of steep rocky uphill climb ahead of me, mist rolling in from across the valley to my side. Alarm bells chimed in my head.

There were other hikers on the trail, but most who had left El Chileno at approximately the same time as me had forged ahead at a much quicker pace. Perhaps they recognized the viewing window of time was limited. I hadn't even thought to ask about weather conditions when I checked in to claim bunk and backpack storage. Without question, those passing me by were experienced hikers. I was not.

Standing in a small crook on the trail, that voice of reason which nudges in a whisper was telling me to make the turnaround now...head back down and away from the rolling mist. Climbing up, although tiring, was always easier for me than coming back down a steep incline. My feet, always placed gingerly, tentatively, once poles were planted, was my method. Slow. Quite slow, but it worked. I knew the trek down would likely be at a slower pace until I reached the point where the creek bed leveled. One last look to the hikers well ahead of me, now faded in distance and fog, and the decision was confirmed.

As anticipated, the hike down presented challenges as I fought to find solid footing on now wet rock faces along the path. The moisture in the air, not rain but mist, had brought a slickness to the surfaces not there thirty minutes earlier. Astonished at the beauty of encroaching mist against the granite cliffs I stopped often, taking in the sight, assured I had made the appropriate decision in choosing to retreat.

Step by step, rock by rock, my confidence began to settle. Voices in the distance let me know I was not alone and I opted to pick up speed if only a very little bit. Mistake! Planting my right foot squarely on what looked to be a flat dry slab of granite, down I slipped, poles askew, a panicked cry escaping as I slid to a stop a few feet away, lying on my pack.

Gingerly I wiggled my feet; all good. Wrists, a tad sore, bent easily as I tested for injury. Sitting up slowly, although shook at the sudden fall, I knew all was well and I had escaped injuries in this slide down the path.

"Hey, are you okay?" came a shout from somewhere further up the incline. "Are you hurt?"

Deep breath. "I'm fine. I'm not hurt." I yelled back, voice a tad shaky.

As I slowly pulled myself up, a young couple, experienced in maneuvering steep rocky trails, appeared around the corner.

"You sure you're okay?" they questioned.

"Fine. Really. Just slid. I'm not hurt. Bruised ego perhaps." I grinned as they nearly ran past.

How did they do that? Literally, they were bounding down the hillside, no poles, completely at ease. Mountain goats in their element!

Checking my watch, I started back down the creek bed. Even with slow and careful footing, the descent took less time than anticipated. I reached the more level surface and took a deep sigh of relief. And, as quickly as it had rolled in, the mist began to dissipate allowing a much less concerned trek back down to El Chileno.

Funny, I had walked over five hundred miles a few months earlier and not once taken a tumble. In fact, I remember being so aware of solid footing on the Camino because stubbing a toe, or taking a mild stumble as Jack and I walked our black lab, Lucky in the park, had become the norm. In an attempt to discern the increase in tripping, I had even Googled possible physical problems that may be the cause. I seemed to trip over something every day. Google anything and there will be 101 possible scenarios for any given physical ailment. How to worry yourself sick!

In the end, after a clean, clear five hundred miles across northern Spain, I decided that my continual catching of my toe on a tree root stub or slightly raised paver stone was, in fact, a physiological expression of my tripping in life. Tripping in a marriage that was no longer working. It may sound odd, but it made sense.

I knew things needed to change, yet I was continually allowing the status quo in my marriage. I refused to face head on the changes that needed to occur. By the time my Camino was underway, the decision to divorce had been made, my personal things had been shipped back to the States from Spain, and the next chapter of my life had begun. And, no more continual tripping. It was over. Yesterday's slide, the first slip or trip in many months, was simply that: a wet rock and loose footing. But, it left me aware. Yesterday's tumble reminded me to stay focused on the positive and move forward.

That was yesterday. Now, on this glorious new morning, los Torres and El Chileno are behind me and los Cuernos lies ahead in the next four to five hours. The mist of the early morning has dissipated and I am treated, once again, to a view of turquoise Lago Nordenskjold decorating the valley below.

It is going to be an amazing day in Patagonia!

CHAPTER NINE

Walking with E!

"Are you listening? asked the Universe.
"I am Aware. I am Receptive. I am Accepting,"
answered Me.

"Shirl, use your poles, like I used my canes...out in front, lean into them."

I hear her familiar voice...*feel* it really. E, letting me know she is right here with me, walking with me. Her words, a comfortable knowing that I have the strength needed, the tools required, to bring me down this last turning slope into the final stretch before arriving at los Cuernos camp for the night. Deep in the mountains of Patagonian Chile, she finds me and touches my heart with her words.

This day has been wonderfully slow, not arduous in any manner. So why now the wobbly legs? The returned fear of a tumble during these last three kilometers? It has been five hours of casual walking. The well-worn path has been smooth for the most of the day. Ascents and descents have been limited and quite short in nature. And it has been quiet, so mystically serenely quiet.

I've stopped many times to soak in the scenery. Gratitude stops. Sit... breathe deep...thank the Universe for the beauty surrounding me. Thankful for the quiet. Thankful for the strength and health I feel as I walk these scenic paths of the famous W Trek in southern Chile. Groups of hikers move past. I step aside, bid them good day, listen as their voices fade around the next bend. My space once again.

So why does this final short descent affect me? It is in this abnormal moment of unsteadiness that E's spirit reaches me. She calls me by name with her instructions: "Shirl! Use your poles like I used my canes...out in front, lean into them."

Have you ever *felt* the words of someone you have loved...someone who has died, yet seems present? The vibration of their voice becomes a river of energy meandering through every blood vessel, soaking every cell. Sound and feeling...one sense. Validation that everything is here and now. Sound, touch, sight...they blend together as words meld into the body. And here is E. Her spirit comes to let me know this is to be *our* adventure. Shirl (me) and E off again, together, discovering...living.

Today is Feb 19th, the third anniversary of the last days of her life.

Three years ago today, I sat with her daughters as we cried, accepting that her life was ending. An oxygen tube down her throat...a machine pumping air into a tired and broken body...prolonging a death that is due. On this day, three years ago, the grating, noisy tube is removed, releasing her from pain. She is finally being released from the multiple sclerosis crippling her back...her hands...her brain. Released from lungs that no longer fill with enough air...eyes which fight to see. Released...into the glorious freedom of the next world...a world in which her spirit is reborn. A world in which she runs along her beloved ocean beaches, waves licking at feet that can feel again...sand, seafoam...life!

On this anniversary of her last days, as I trek the W trails of Torres del Paine in southern Chile, she comes to me with a voice clear and strong...a voice pulsing through every fiber of my being. Calling me by my nickname, Shirl, she lets me know she is with me. Names we gave each other many years before, I am Shirl and her, E, Ethel. Shirley and Ethel, alter egos to Kate and MJ, sisters by heart...aunt and niece by birth. These personas, Shirl and E, have no physical restrictions. These two women are completely unaware of the ravages of MS on MJ's body. E and Shirl, dearest friends...strong, fun, flirting with life!

"Shirl, if I can do Puerto Vallarta, you can do this!"

Once again I catch my breath as she reaches me from somewhere beyond. Words, warm, hugging my heart. She takes me back twelve years.

It was the year MJ turned fifty. A milestone birthday for most, especially sacred to her as she had fought illness for so many years. A life of health and financial issues had kept any foreign travel simply a dream. MJ was turning fifty, and I was in a position to splurge. Off we flew to Puerto Vallarta, Mexico, January 5th, her day. One glorious week of a winter warm-up complete with shopping, lounging, and a swim-up pool bar...heaven! E and Shirl, the alter egos, on vacation in paradise.

When the physical body needs a break, when the soul needs filling to keep the body going, amazing changes can occur. She went on that adventure in a body reliant on walking canes. And, as life happens, she sported a walking cast, the result of a recent fall which cracked her ankle. With the doctor's permission, and a spirit that simply would not consider the alternative, E hobbled her wracked body onto the plane. I swear to this day, the MS went dormant and the ankle temporarily mended. For the next five days, E was able to swim, wander the shops and walk the beach shopping for that perfect souvenir ring. She ate with hands able to grasp fork and knife. She slept soundly at night and woke ready to take in each new day.

One afternoon torrents of rain brought flooded streets. We were in the heart of old town Puerto Vallarta. As in any land that experiences regular flash flooding, the sidewalk curbs were high. Where a normal step up may be six inches, these curbs must have measured twelve inches in height. With her cane, for safety, and her walking cast...up and down those curbs she stepped. On and off sidewalks as we dodged cars spraying gallons of water in their wake. Off to a favorite bar haunt to wait out the downpour. Off to celebrate being alive and *living!*

Twelve years later, here in Patagonia on February 19th, her lively angel spirit speaks to me. I will do the walking and she will guide me through the rough stretches giving strength and support. Angel wings on my legs!

So many glorious memories flood my heart and head. As we traverse the landscape, I talk with E. I chat about current life, speak of her daughters and grandchildren...share my immense appreciation of the landscape unfolding before us. And I share memories of long ago...memories tucked away in my younger mind.

She is MJ, my aunt and elder by only four years. How I envied her! She grew up as a single child...no others to steal away attention and affection. No other children usurping limited financial resources. She had new clothes and, what seemed to me—a young girl living on welfare—a life of luxury. So very far from the truth, but to my young eyes she lived a princess life! Her own bedroom complete with a cushioned window seat overlooking a grassy front lawn. I was a ten-year-old welfare girl from the projects longing for a *real* house. A ten-year-old, the eldest, wishing for less responsibility in a family of five children. My Mom had five little ones while attending college, earning a teaching degree. We managed on welfare housing and the government food trucks of the 1960s. And me, well, I did what the eldest does: helped to watch over four younger ones.

MJ's life, one I shared for two weeks in the summers of 1965 and 1966, was my dream. She was fourteen, a young teenager in a neighborhood she had lived in all of her life. Popular, she had girlfriends...and *boys*! She wore a light lip gloss that she applied so delicately in the bathroom mirror. I perched, spellbound, on the toilet seat, watching. Long dark hair, dimples that grew threefold when she grinned...she was my definition of pretty. And me? Red hair, freckles, too tall for my years, cat eye glasses and chipped front teeth. Yes, I was understandably bewitched by my Auntie MJ.

Three years later, MJ came to visit us for the summer in Port Angeles, our new home. Mom had finished her degree and taken her first teaching position. MJ and I joined with other kids from Port Angeles, taking busses to the berry fields each day.

Strawberries, raspberries...we worked all day picking, relishing the opportunity to make some money. We laughed, we played, we stayed up watching late night talk shows on the weekends. MJ became the big sister I never had. She was with us only a short while that summer, but the bond between us grew deep. Then back to Spokane she went.

The following year she came again, this time to act as babysitter while Mom took classes to complete her required fifth year teacher studies. MJ was so grown up! I was a fourteen-year-old teenager while she had become a young woman. I picked berries again, but this year babysitting the others kept her at home. When I hopped off the bus, however, she was waiting to sit and chat with me...hear my stories of the day. We shared popcorn and 7-UP, giggling as the vapors wafted up our noses when we popped the bottle caps. We stayed up late after the younger ones were tucked in bed. She was my best friend during those summers. She was so very beautiful while I had become the quintessential "geeky looking girl" complete with a height of 5'11"...at age fourteen!

A year later, she was nineteen years old and getting married. Now fifteen, I once again perched on the toilet seat in my grandparents' old home on Mallon Avenue in Spokane. This was the house that four years earlier had seemed a mansion. As I sat and watched, mesmerized as she carefully applied the cosmetics of a soon to be bride, I saw smallness. I saw the chipped paint and tiny old-fashioned cupboards of a tired bathroom. My grandparents' mansion was simply an aged home in an older, run-down neighborhood. MJ, however, was still the stunning beauty I always saw!

Voices ahead of me pull me back to the present. E and I keep our distance. How can one reflect on the glories of this inspiring nature with voices echoing across the fields? Yet, my heart is light. My soul knows E is walking with me, guiding me over the slippery portions; helping my tired legs. And then my soul hears her again:

"Your legs are your wings. Mine didn't work, yours do."

I don't recall when I first learned she was ill. Somewhere in the fog of memory, I know she was diagnosed with Lupus in her late twenties or early thirties. Her mobility was not that of someone her age. Hands did not grip properly...markers of what lie ahead. During those years, we lived different adult lives with husbands, babies, and challenges each of our own. When we saw each other, however, it was always joyous, reminiscent of those teenage years laughing over 7-UP vapors and stories of the summer silliness we shared.

Years passed. MJ's body failed her bit by bit. She lived an adult life heavily encumbered. One problem solved and another surfaced: health, financial, and child related. Always she faced such challenges. I agonized over why one woman was given such a life of hardship. Why there never seemed to be a break in challenges? Yet through it all, through every month of every year as life grew more and more difficult, she found humor. MJ not only laughed, she had a wicked sense of humor that brought tears to my eyes. My laughter, so intense I doubled over... barely able to breathe. And in her reflective times, MJ found joy...'magic moments' she called them. Moments of peace...moments of joy surpassing the pain.

And now, as we walk a path circumventing ancient lakes, gazing at jagged mountain peaks, handsaw teeth in the skies, E reminds me of the years I brought mementos from my travels. Memory bags from faraway lands. Coasters from a first drink on a vacation in Budapest; entry tickets to the Haggia Sophia in Istanbul; menu covers from Oktoberfest in Munich. Each trip I collected a memory bag for MJ...for E! She said they took her to foreign lands she wished to see; they allowed her to escape her bed and travel once again, as we had years prior on that birthday in Mexico. She reminds me now how much it was appreciated...she tells me she is so truly grateful to be able to walk this adventure with me.

Tears flow...loss, happiness, laughter, heartache...flowing down my cheeks.

MJ died three years ago. When I entered her hospital room, she was on a life support. Pneumonia, brought about by MS complications, was claiming her. Unable to talk, semiconscious, the nurses suggested I speak with her anyway...have her wiggle a toe when she heard me. In the depths of ethers, that state of in-between this physical world we call home and the welcoming center of love we call death, E found her way and gave me, her Shirl, the slightest of toe wiggles. E and Shirl together for one more adventure in this life...together as she left for the next. Her adventure this time...she would be the one sending mementos and messages.

I now understand: MJ had *faith*. She did not use the word faith, yet she lived a belief that everything would work out. She *knew* she would have what she needed when she needed it. I think she also knew that life events happen in precisely the order in which they are meant. We didn't speak of it as such, but I believe she somehow trusted that the Universe was working with her: where finances would come from, how her legs would work when she needed them most, how her girls would handle her death when that time came.

She may not have known in a logical, rational sense, but she *knew*. Her soul knew and in this she taught me about faith; what it meant to surrender to what is and simply *trust*. Her spirit reminds me to let go...let the Universe unfold...and simply watch and listen as it whispers.

And here in Patagonia, in this place where the energy of the earth seeps through every fiber of my being, I feel her assuring me all will be well...surrender and trust.

"Your legs are your wings...."

CHAPTER TEN

Lexy Ann

"Tell me about forgiveness," prompted the Universe.
"I can do that," answered Me.

The chilled cerveza hits my parched throat and burns at first swallow. Refugio los Cuernos. I have reached los Cuernos after a deeply emotional day. MJ's words linger in my head. "Your legs are your wings. Yours work, mine didn't." I love her. I miss her.

Alone in the refugio dining hall, vacant except for the few straggling trekkers coming to check in and claim their bunks, I feel lost in a cavern of emptiness.

The day has been long and tiring, even though astounding in its beauty. I have been whisked into a lifetime of memories as MJ's spirit settled in to walk this walk with me today.

"Use your poles" she offered. "Out in front, like I used my canes." Her voice wrapped around my heart, and although an initial surprise, it felt surprisingly normal. I have become used to receiving guiding messages from loved ones who have passed to the next realm. Jeannie, Sis... this has been going on for years. MJ had been with me before. This was not her first visit.

I first came to understand the connection we have with those who have left after my mother-in-law, Sis' death in 2007. She and I had been so close, chosen friends after several years of dancing a not-so-pretty dance between daughter-in-law and mother-in-law. In the end, we had negotiated terms and recognized we had far more to gain in our relationship if we allowed it. Stop fighting. Stop the defensiveness. We were not in competition for Jack. He was her son, my husband. We loved him differently and could love him together.

Sis died after battling years of colon cancer. Her final eighteen months were spent with Jack and me, in our home, in the Seattle area. A native of Munich, Germany, yet American by passport as she had married Jack's Dad, an American Army officer, she had opted to come live with us. When the final choices became a type of assisted living/nursing facility in Munich, or home to Seattle where her children lived, where she could be loved and cared for in the warmth of a home she already knew, she chose to come to the States. Many visits over the years had brought friendships between her and my family, as well as our neighborhood 'Friday afternoon bar buddies.' It would be the perfect solution and she jumped at it. Five days after making the decision, we were in flight to Seattle.

Eighteen months later, she lost her battle. After several days waking in the early morning hours, looking at me and questioning why she was still here, she quietly passed away into her new realm. Jack sat by her side whispering his goodbyes in German, their native tongue. He held her, reminding her that her lifelong girlfriends who had already gone before were waiting for her with

Champagne and Rummikub tiles so they might share lazy afternoons giggling, as girlfriends do, once again.

Within a very short time, Sis began showing herself to me in the form of 11s—7:11, 9:11...license plates with 11s—all at specific moments in time as I was debating significant questions or concerns. There she would be. It had taken me several weeks to realize what was happening, but once I did, I knew I could count on her for guidance when I stumbled in decisions. She is with me still, eight years later, each and every day. Mary Jo coming to me as my legs tired and my feet lost solid footing today, was not unusual. It just happens.

Outside, a large open deck serves as the gathering place as hikers arrive for the night. Groups of two, four, six...friends experiencing the adventure of this famous W Trek gather together. They look so young. Am I crazy? Alone, a woman of fifty-seven with only the claim of the Camino? These hikers have climbed the mountains of Nepal, Kilimanjaro, Mount Everest...I claim only a very long walk.

She asks if she can join me. A young woman, long sun-kissed blonde hair swinging loose under her colorful headband.

"Of course," I say, pulling a stool from beneath the table. "Hi, I'm Lexy Ann," she smiles.

For the next four hours, over dinner and into the evening, we chat. Lexy Ann, twenty-four, confidence oozing, shares her adventures. She has come to Chile to teach English. Her experience teaching English as a second language in her native San Diego area has led her to believe this might be the perfect situation, at least for the time being. Students in San Diego, some from Chile, have offered housing with their families in the major city of Santiago should she decide to stay. Lexy Ann has given herself eight months to determine her next moves. She chose the W Trek, days alone in the serene beauty of the Chilean mountains, to release herself from all other obligations and make some decision about the 'what's next' in her world.

"No, no job yet," she says. "I will hike and then decide where I'll teach."

I hear in her voice a calm; a complete confidence that all will be well. No fear, completely at peace with the knowledge that if she simply allows herself time and space the answers will come. What a wise soul! Twenty-four years old and she already knows what it has taken me years to learn: Trust, accept, and the Universe will conspire on your behalf.

We talk travel, of course. She is amazed at my having completed a five-hundred mile walk across northern Spain— French Pyrenees to the Atlantic Ocean.

Me, in awe at a young woman who has already traveled Nepal on her own, with only backpack and trust.

And we talk about synchronicities, those whispers of truth available when we learn to listen. I share my story of knowing I was to walk the Camino, the marriage years and my love for Jack, although now that union has been left behind. I share the messages received from my angels, Jeannie, my sister, Sis and MJ.

Funny, I still say left behind...as though it is. So sure I have concluded the heartache. Yet catching myself in simple phrases, aware that there is more release to come. An ongoing process after twenty years.

She shares of her anger and blame at a father, her hero, destroying their family through an affair with a coworker. Her father, her protector, her model of all that is good and right in a father and husband. Her mother left shattered, shamed. Lexy Ann, as most daughters, felt the need to protect her Mom. Questions of *why* were not asked; she was too young. Dad had committed the ultimate betrayal and that was all there was to it.

Years later when her mother shared a deeper truth of their marriage, an intimacy craved by her father, an intimacy withheld, Lexy realized her anger must be set free. Now as a grown woman herself, a deeper understanding of human relations in marriage prods her to forgive.

"It had been ten years, time to open the doors and reconnect with my Dad. I am still unhappy about his choice, but at least now I understand. And, I can love him."

I am mesmerized as she tells my story.

Off she wanders to purchase us two more cervezas.

Christmas. I am seventeen years old. Head over heels in love with the commercial fisherman who has stolen my heart, I attend his local church, a Friends Church; Evangelical Quaker might be an appropriate description. A born again Christian, this man is kind, loving and solid in his new found beliefs. And I am in love with him. Heart and soul open, I begin reading the Bible daily, joining him for church and worship classes, understanding the concept of testimony within the church.

Raised by a single mom, a mother to five of us, I now understand in a greater light the delicacies of my mother's and father's marriage. But, all those growing up years, I felt he was the one and only cause of our situation, and much as I loved my Daddy, my anger grew through the years.

Immediately following their divorce were years of welfare housing, food truck government handouts and growing up quickly in terms of responsibility as the eldest of the five. My Mom, faced with needing to supply for her family, managed to earn a teaching degree at the local college. Four years as she balanced her education and a family of five little ones, ages eight years down to one year. Extremely limited funds tested her skills. In awe. I am still in awe of her perseverance. I am in awe of her ability to create joyous memories through infinitely trying times. I am in awe of her love.

As the years passed and we managed to move forward in life, she accepted her first teaching post and we moved to the beautiful town of Port Angeles, on the Olympic Peninsula of Washington State. Mountains and water surrounded us. As a little girl from the arid regions of eastern Washington, desert country, I was in heaven. Yet, financial hardships remained and the older I got the more I blamed my father. I saw it as his fault; I was unable to view anything different. How dare my stepsister live what seemed a life of luxury, while we were so limited. By the time I was in my early teens, I chose minimal contact.

And then, at seventeen years old, with a newfound belief in Christianity and the practices of open witness within my church family, I found myself forgiving. It was not a conscious decision to forgive—it just happened. Whatever the story, whatever the circumstances, it no longer mattered. What mattered was that I reach out to my father, that I open the door I had slammed shut and go to him.

The Christmas I was seventeen, I flew to Montana and spent the holiday with my Dad, stepmom, and stepsister. Christmas is incredibly important in my family. That I chose to leave then hurt my Mom deeply. And I knew it, but there was no option. It was time, and I had to go.

Never once have I looked back; never once have I questioned what my soul knew I was to do. My father and I have had a beautiful relationship ever since. I am grateful.

Dinner that night is shared in this same open dining room with a group of about fifty hikers spending the night at los Cuernos Refugio. The room ripples with laughter and excited chatter, as benches are slid together to seat us all. As we dive into steaming pots of lentil and ham soup, hunks of home-style bread, and family style platters of lasagna, one of the refugio workers grabs his guitar, saunters to the lone seat by picture windows overlooking the lakes below and hushes the crowd with a haunting voice. Carbohydrates for the belly, lullaby vocals for the spirit...we will sleep tonight!

CHAPTER ELEVEN

Glacier Frances

"If you could heal yourself of one negative trait,
what would it be?" asked the Universe.
"I would learn to release passing judgement," answered Me.

Slept, I slept deeply last night, so soundly. Perhaps the carbohydrates of a filling pasta meal, quite probably the haunting guitar lullaby as our entertainer played later into the night out on the front deck area just beyond the dorm room window.

Breakfast tables are being set in place as I tuck nighttime belongings back in my pack and wander into the hallway. Hikers, sleepy eyed, hair standing on end, search for the bathrooms. Large, communal bathrooms—there are two that I see—provide a multitude of sinks, three or four shower stalls, and toilet facilities. With everyone preparing for their day within the same sixty to ninety-minute window, crowds and waiting are expected. I am pleasantly surprised at grabbing a sink, with a small mirror, as I walk through the door.

As on the Camino, early morning preparations for the day are a relatively quick project. Shove my head under the sink faucet, wet my hair a bit, and stir it into place. (Thanks Mom for the lovely curls) Brush my teeth, do a quick spit bath of sorts with disposable wipes and out the door I go. No makeup. This trip is about sunscreen at these altitudes and loads of it! Showers, for me, take place at the end of the walk day as soon as my bunk is assigned. With other hikers joining in groups as their walk day ends, a solo hiker such as myself has pretty much free reign over shower facilities. It worked well on the Camino; it works great here in Patagonia!

Today's hike will be a long one. From here at Refugio los Cuernos, I will be hiking into Valle Frances, toward the mirador for Glacier Frances and then back down the valley and on toward the Refugio at Paine Grande. The photos of tonight's accommodations show an enormous hotel style facility with cafeteria buffet food service and several wings of dorm rooms. Additionally, a camping area offers placement for tents for those hearty souls doing the full outdoor adventure.

One day perhaps; not this time! Total mileage will be twenty-five and three-tenths kilometers.

The difficulty today is ranked as one of the tougher days given the hike up and into the valley. But oh the reward—French Glacier! I heard others chatting about it last night. They felt it was a hike highlight. I am anxious to get underway!

The crowds are gathering. A hearty breakfast of oatmeal with cream, toasted bread and jam, hard-boiled eggs, orange juice, and coffee greets us. Glancing around the room, I see a hand waving me over. Lexy Ann is settled in with a group she had met a day or two before.

"Hey, come here. There's room right there across from me!"

I slide in, introductions coming from all sides. One of the greatest joys of the walking is the camaraderie with happy souls. Be it Camino walkers or hikers, everyone seems to sense the '*oneness*' of us all. Energy is positive. A perfect start to the day.

A kettle of steaming oatmeal is passed my way. Family style is the norm—easier and certainly less wasteful—as hikers take what they will eat and pass it along. Oatmeal from a kettle; how long has it been?

6:00 AM and Mom's voice calls up the stairs. "Wake up kids...time to get up. Good morning."

My alarm will ring in a couple of minutes. It's a school morning and that means hustle. This morning getting the oatmeal cooked is my job. I hate oatmeal. I despise oatmeal. Oh the luxury of pastries, sausages, boxes of sugary yummy cereal...anything would be better than oatmeal. With five kids, however, a hot bowl of oatmeal and some toast is the more cost effective way to get full tummies out the door on time!

I am fourteen. A teenager and very proud of that fact! Second in command to my Mom, she often lets me handle the oatmeal production as she preps for school herself. One teacher and five kids out the door by 7:20 AM.

Quaker Oats. The real stuff, not packages of the sugary instant variety mixed with water and into the microwave. Quaker Oats in a pot we have had all my life. Heavy grey metal with a strange diveted outer finish, this pot cooks morning oatmeal, pops buttery Friday night popcorn, simmers slumgullion (hamburger, macaroni noodles and tomato sauce; cheap food to feed many young mouths). This well-used pot feeds us. No, it is not the only pot, just the favorite. It's the right size for this family of six. It is my favorite pot. It has been around as long as me!

On the table it goes—family style. Help yourself! A touch of sugar and a dash of cinnamon hide the taste of the powdered milk we mix in a large pitcher. I will be truly rich when I can drink milk from a carton! For now, powdered milk. At least it is the Milkman powdered milk and no longer the horrid government issued stuff from the food trucks. We nicknamed government issued milk 'blue milk' for its lack of consistency and watery color. Milkman is a step toward 'real' milk - milk in a carton from the grocery store. One day...one day!

Someone next to me passes down a large pewter cream pitcher. I tip it. Rich, thick milk pours over my piping hot oatmeal. A dish cradling small dollops of butter makes its way to the end where I am seated. Helping myself, I plop a scoop dead center of my bowl. Butter melts across the cereal oozing to the sides. Oatmeal...fortification. Heaven! I no longer hate oatmeal.

* * * *

Boom! The sound echoes across the enclosed valley. This gorge, surrounded by the granite of the Paine Massif, reverberates as a freshly calved chunk of French Glacier falls to the ground somewhere below. The river, running alongside and just below the trail, rushes over boulders, cascading into crystalline pools. As I ascend deeper into the hills toward French Glacier, I see hikers are taking a break along the glacial pools that have formed near the river's edge. Tempted as I am to descend the steep climb to the water, my smarter self jumps in:

"No Kate. Just walk. No need to take on extra risks...your day will be full enough."

Granite boulders, which once crashed down the hills from above, form a blockade to the natural progression of the path. Signage seems misleading. If I follow the signs, the haul over boulders will be significant. A twenty-pound pack on my back, I find myself questioning the route, questioning my abilities. And most certainly, I am slowing a group behind me.

"Step aside, let them pass. Deep breath...just go slow." MJ whispers in my ear, in my heart. She joined me yesterday, her angel words giving me strength when legs were weak. She hikes with me again today as I make the climb.

As the final two hikers in the group pass ahead of me, I have stepped aside to allow them to pass, the woman halts at the next climb. Unsure of her footing, her husband, I will later learn, offers a hand as she tucks trekking poles in one arm and he leads her through the maze of rocks to the path above. Watching me assess the situation, he steps around her offering a hand.

"Here you go, grab my hand if you need to. Just put your feet where I tell you. Tuck your poles under one arm and use your hands. You'll be able to pull yourself up."

Following his words, I am soon on the path above and ready to move on. Ohhhh, the coming down though! This will be a challenge.

Three days ago, at the beginning of this five-day hike, I found myself purposefully taking my time as I hiked the trails above Lago Nordenskiold. It was a day of gratitude. A day in which each turn provoked such intense appreciation for the spectacular scenery; for the serene quiet. Short steep climbs had come easily. Climb, rest...walk some more, rest. All in perfect timing.

Heart shaped rocks, my 'prayer rocks,' were plentiful. Each one prompted me to focus for several minutes on a loved one, sending a wish to the Universe for their safety, well-being, and especially that they be blessed with a joyful day. Amazing how many heart shaped rocks lie at our feet when we take a moment to search the path we walk. Gifts from the Universe reminding us that love...love is the key to everything.

Hikers passing whispered a quiet "Buenas días" with the nod of their heads. We recognized the spiritual nature of where we were in the world, honoring the blessings bestowed in the glorious land with quiet reverence. Anything louder than a hushed whisper came from nature herself as deep in the mountains glaciers cracked, their sounds of losing a piece of themselves a cry, a howl into the skies.

Rounding a bend in the trail, the 180-degree view of Lago Nordenskjold below, her aquamarine waters shimmering in the midday sun, loud harsh voices filled the air. English, American English, as a group of hikers posed together for their memory photo above the lake. Gathering on a promontory, they yelled to each other to take places. Women, shrill grating voices shouting and laughing, sounds echoing across the fields above the lake.

Nerves immediately on end, I stopped dead in my tracks, realizing that to keep walking now would have me just ahead of them in the final kilometers of the day. My peaceful meditative walk would be left far behind as I listened to booming voices, minor profanities ringing shrill in the air. As their plan involved several minutes of maneuvering for the perfect photo, I opted to retreat around the bend, drop my pack and quietly wait out their photo break. Loud. Noisy, crass Americans in total disregard of the unspoken pact to share this land quietly. Selfish and disrespectful; I felt embarrassed at their actions, embarrassed to be countrymen.

And now, here I sit in stunned awe listening to the glacier beyond the cut creak and moan as it prepares to calve. Ice shatters, breaking in immense chucks, crashing to the rushing river below. A group of eight is seated several feet away, quietly eating their box lunch, as am I. Their voices whisper as they take turns passing someone's professional camera to each other posing for memory photos.

Setting my ciabatta sandwich aside for a moment, I wander across the viewpoint and ask, using the universal hand signal of pointing to the camera and clicking my thumb and forefinger together, if they would like a group shot. "Un foto? Todo ustedes?" My Spanish is minimal at best.

One of the men reaches an arm into the air gesturing to someone behind me to come join.

I am given the "wait just a moment" motion as the American couple who helped me over the final climb come into view and join the group.

Laughing, we say a quick hello and introductions are given. No need for Spanish. These are Americans and I now realize they are the same group I so judged a few days ago. Yes, they had been loud in those moments. And how quickly I had judged them for far more than the thirty minutes of revelry I witnessed. I am embarrassed; no, I am ashamed. I snap a group shot they deem perfect and head back to my lunch. I don't ask to join them, nor do they make an invite. They recognize my need for solitude...or is it penance?

Several minutes later, lunch break over, as they are preparing to leave, they give me the 'come along' hand motion, waving me into their group.

"The climb down is steep, you are better to be with someone. Hike down with us! Join us for the rest of the day if you want." George, who I later learn is the group leader, has welcomed me and offered a much-needed safety net.

An hour later, at the bottom of the climb, where the path now cuts across a wooden bridge traversing the rushing water below, we say our good-byes. For me, I offer my heartfelt thankyous for their kindness and consideration in seeing me down the hill. From this point on I am certain of the route, certain of terrain, and most certain that I am due at the confessional of the Universe!

CHAPTER TWELVE

Lago Grey

"Do you have the fortitude, Kate?
Will you carry on?" asked the Universe.
"I think so...no, I know so," answered a determined Me.

As hikers gather in the immense cafeteria of Refugio Paine Grande, filling tummies with an assortment of bakery treats, hot scrambled eggs and the ever-present oatmeal, I opt for coffee and a mini-baguette with butter.

Last night's delightful culinary dinner offerings here at Paine Grande was a heavenly treat. So many options. Yes, prepared in bulk for the huge crowds, but the options! We all ate far too much.

Thick chunks of bread, sweet butter and homemade jam, the mainstay of breakfasts on my Spanish Camino last year, remain a favorite whenever I travel. Today this mini-baguette slathered with creamy butter reminds me of those days. With steaming hot coffee, it is perfection.

One of the gals I walked with yesterday afternoon, coming down from French Glacier, sits outside the main room doctoring a blistered toe. Coffee mug in hand, I wander out to say good morning. It is a middle toe, the type of blister difficult to protect as a long day wears on. I now have an opportunity to help one of this group who so naturally pulled me into their fold yesterday on the trek down the rocky ravine.

"Good morning! Owww, that one looks painful. How are you set for bandages?" I ask.

"Well, I have small ones left, but they really are not thick enough. I will have to double them up to protect it I think."

"Hold on!" I offer. "I have just the thing. A great toe bandage I found last year while hiking the Camino in Spain. I have a few with me and haven't needed them this trip. Be right back!"

My pack is waiting for me near the side door where I dropped it before the hunt for morning coffee. Pulling a cushy silicone toe sleeve bandage from my zip lock baggie of medical goodies, I make an offering that I know will ease the pain and pressure for the remainder of the day.

Funny, a small silicone bandage has brought a warm heartfelt hug cementing a connection between two hikers who, until yesterday, could have passed each other without ever a greeting. A hug I will now hold as my reminder against harsh judgement, as this young lady was one of the loud Americans I admonished as their voices echoed across the silent valley three days ago. I stand grateful for a chance to help, humbled that my penance is so simple.

* * * *

Lago Grey and Grey Glacier are the end point today. Two more days of walking in this mysterious, captivating land and it will be back to a rattly bus and the city. But, that is two days from now. Today I will focus completely on the glory that surrounds me: the majestic grey peaks, capped in volcanic black, winds whipping harsh in the open spaces of the walk.

I have not felt these winds since my initial arrival to Torres del Paine National Park several days ago.

Now, full backpack and uphill grade, they challenge me to continue.

"Show us, Kate. Show us what you are made of. Can you do this? Sure you don't want to turn around and just go back. No one would know. You're tired. It's okay." Whistling wind assaults my ears with its teasing taunts.

No, I have come this far and I will make it all the way to Refugio Grey, just as planned.

This is only wind. I have gone through this before in the Pyrenees between Orisson and Roncesvalles on the Camino Frances. Day Two of my Camino, seventy kilometers per hour winds buffeted our packs, threatening to send us rolling into huddled herds of sheep bunkered down in the grassy hillside. I learned to lower my head and plant my poles for support then; I will do the same now.

A bend in the trail an hour later and the buffeting subsides. For a short time at least, I am in protected territory. This valley I am trekking today, known for its galing winds, is offering me the full on experience of hiking it in all its glory. Slower going for sure, but that's okay. I'm in no hurry. As always, I step aside just off the trail as the more nimble hikers race past. Slightly jealous of their agility, I still have no desire to hurry this journey to completion. Muffled voices fade into the wind as they round the next bend up ahead.

Off to my right a signpost beckons. Laguna del Patos. Laguna del Patos, the imposing peaks of the snow-capped Andes far to the west, sits serenely quiet, nestled in a protected valley. Waters, a mirror to brilliant blue skies, reflect wind swept trees from the adjacent slopes.

Tossing my jacket to the ground for protection, I tuck in behind an immense granite boulder, the vista spread before me. I have found a quiet sun-soaked corner of the world to settle for a mid-morning break. Eerily quiet, others seem to have bypassed this stop altogether. I am being gifted, blessed with such incredible beauty in these moments of solitude — these moments of connection with the energy of the Universe. And I am filled with a deep sense of humble gratitude.

As if Laguna de Patos was not enough for a day, another one and a half kilometers along the path I am greeted with my first vista of the immense nineteen kilometer-glacier that is Glacier Grey, one of three in the Southern Patagonian Ice Field. Breathtaking, the glacier's edge stretches across Lago Grey, ice blue towers, dangerously long shards of broken mirror, slicing upwards to the vast sky above. Again, the Earth in all its majesty takes my breath away. Several of us stand in complete silence, utter awe, as we shake our heads silently at this unbelievable beauty before us.

* * * *

The final hour of the day has been filled with moments of wonder as I walk through fields of lavender, magenta, ivory and pink-toned foxglove, colors magnified in the filtering sunlight. The stalks stand over five feet tall reaching for the sun beyond the lenga forest I am traversing. The rushing water of a mountain stream far below the footbridge I cross gathers strength as it spills crystal clear over a rocky ledge into Lago Grey, now off to my right as I maneuver the final descents.

Steep paths lined by jagged rocky cuts form a narrow passage, the only passage, leading to the valley floor. If I am to make these turns, not take a misstep, once again it will be wise to toss all modesty to the wind. My decision: simply settle my fanny on the boulders, working my way slowly down to the path below. Graceful? Hardly! Practical? Absolutely. That I slow the others, confident in the placement of their feet, well, so be it.

And that is how I descend this final climb: on my butt, poles tucked under my arms, hands and feet placed squarely on solid surface. Boulder by boulder to the bottom of the ravine. Charming!

Standing up, brushing off my backside, I smile and apologize to anyone behind me. I made it. I made it on my own and I am not too proud to claim it! Deep breath. I will never see these people again in my life, right? Except maybe at dinner tonight. Oh well.

Refugio Grey is remarkably quiet when I arrive. One of the last to check in, I expect a much larger crowd. Activities promoted at the front counter answer the question. Those who passed me by have claimed bunks and gone to kayak Lago Grey, a trip which will take them to the glacier's edge. Grey Glacier, nineteen kilometers in extension, is immense. Breathtaking. And for those on the kayak cruise, just a quarter mile in front of them. Any closer is far too dangerous as icebergs calve into the lake.

Others have opted for the ice trekking adventure on the glacier itself. Avid outdoors mountaineering types would be remiss to come to Patagonia and not hike one of the glacier trekking adventures available.

My bunk this final night is in a room of only four beds. Two up, two down. Although backpacks are tossed on the bottom two, claimed by earlier arrivals, no one else is present. A purple REI quick-dry towel, just like mine, hangs from a hook on the wall. Well, someone has had a shower before heading back out on their afternoon adventure.

Unpacking my bag, digging for a semi-clean pair of pants after my dusty dirty decent on my rear end, the door pops open and in walks a wet-headed Lexy Ann.

"Hi!" We both shout smiling and laughing as a hug ensues.

"Oh I hoped I would see you again, Kate. You just got in?" She is her warm, loving self.

"I did, and am in need of a shower. Are you sticking around or going out?" I ask.

"I am done for the day. That wind was too much. Time to stop, write in my journal, have a beer. Come join me when you're done." We agree.

She heads to the small bar tucked in a corner of the Refugio Grey dining room to snag a cold beer. And me, I head off for a much needed hot shower.

Joining Lexy Ann out on the front veranda of this well-kept and furnished refugio, we catch up on the last couple of days since we saw each other at los Cuernos. She has walked alone during the days, her preference. Evenings have been more filled with people, music and chitchat with fellow hikers. Although we were both at Paine Grande the night before, we managed to miss each other in the hubbub that is the largest of the facilities in the park, catering to a huge tent community as well as the large hostel we had stayed in.

Her plans now are to stay here at Refugio Grey until midday tomorrow. She'll take in the kayaking in the morning and then head back to Paine Grande on the shores of Lago Pehoe for the last afternoon ferry back to park headquarters at 5:00 PM.

As for me, I am shooting for the 12:30 PM ferry to ensure I am at park headquarters in time to catch my shuttle, which will take me to the larger busses. After a transfer at the Chilean/ Argentinian border customs stop, I'll be on my way back to El Calafate. Given the difficulty of some of this day's trek, I will head out by 7.30 AM, after the sun is up a short while, and allow an extra hour for the return hike.

Cold cervezas in hand, we chatter away sharing our impressions of the hike and others we have met. She points out that she and I are the only two solo women hikers on the circuit. Which, and she is one hundred percent right in this, makes us pretty damned cool or genuinely stupid.

Hmmm. I prefer 'pretty damn cool' but am thinking, now that I am in the final hours, genuinely stupid might be more like it. At least for me. She is twenty-four; she is a hiker. Not so this woman!

Either way, we toast to us and our character, that which made us set out to do something like this alone, and call it good!

I ask her if she has made a decision about her next steps. Follow her head and take a position in a Santiago where she has contacts and a potential job, or follow her heart and go toward Valparaiso—make her way, trusting that the Universe will provide. She has decided: Valparaiso it is. We toast. She has made the right decision. When the logic of the head and the pull of one's heart song are at loggerheads, follow the heart. Follow the passion; the rest will follow. She is excited and ready to move forward. My heart sings with her.

A lovely dinner, wine carafes passed person to person, and the evening winds to an end.

The late night star-gazers head out to stretch on the lawn, lose themselves in the mystery of the cosmic alignments above. Lexy Ann joins the group as we say goodnight. For me, time for bed. 7:00 AM will come soon enough, and I feel a sense of trepidation regarding the morning's climb back up my boulder barrier to the path above, which will lead me back to Lago Pehoe and on toward home.

CHAPTER THIRTEEN

Walking

"Your newfound passion, Kate? It has been with you,
tucked deep inside all along," shared the Universe.
"I see it now. She taught me," agreed a delighted Me.

Unable to sleep, it crosses my mind that somehow in the far reaches of Patagonian South America, in a land that has fascinated me since I a young teenager, I am aware that my newfound passion for walking is truly not new at all.

Walking has been an integral part of my world since I was a very little girl. Oh, of course plain and simple walking we all do. I am referring to the grand experiences: the memories evoked of days gone by when a walk became the jumping off to a special occasion, a memory for life. In that journey, that bonding and sharing time as we walked to wherever we might be going, a cell memory is formed. Walking is family. Walking is a special occasion. Walking is joy!

Perhaps because we had very little, perhaps it would have been this way anyway, we walked. A lot. Mom and five kids. We had a car; that wasn't the issue. But, cars cost gas money and we had very little money. And, walking is a bonding time; family time. Walking together brings conversation, teasing, giggles about who did what to whom in a family of five kids. Walking brought silly songs made up as we strolled along singing out the street names, a chance to talk about which trees were which, why the crows lined the telephone lines after a rain, why the grumpy old man who lived on the corner was that way. Walking taught us to watch out for each other.

"Kids, hold hands when we cross. Wait for the light!"

Walking brought us closer to neighbors as we shouted and waved hellos.

Walking was hushed teenage moments whispering my insecurities to Mom. Would I ever be pretty? Would I always be the tallest? Would the boys ever like me? Walking was bonding. Walking was love.

* * * *

After the harsh one-hundred-degree heat of a Spokane summer day begins to dissipate, Mom gathers us together. An evening stroll toward Doyle's Ice Cream Parlor for a late evening treat. Maple trees line the neighborhood sidewalks, branches creating a veil of shade. Older homes, many from the 1900s, once freshly painted and manicured, stately residences, now show cracked peeling paint and worn front steps leading to dandelion lawns.

But, it is the neighborhood of my childhood. My grandparents live here on Mallon Avenue and it is home. A polaroid snapshot forever in my memory. A teenager by this time, the walk is a chance to connect on a more grown up level with Mom while the younger kids run ahead. We walk these sidewalks, content.

* * * *

Easter Sunday, everyone in their Easter dresses and hats, my brother in a sweater and slacks as we walk from our home on Seventh Street, downtown to the local Denny's restaurant on the Port Angeles waterfront for dessert. A walk of about a mile, we are a colorful bunch of Easter candies as parade our way. We hold hands, sing, and chatter on the way to this decadent holiday treat. It is mid-afternoon. The Easter Brunch crowd have all gone home as we pile into the large circular corner booth; plenty of room for the six of us. Menus are handed to each. I am almost twelve and feel quite grown up. Restaurants are an extravagance!

Chocolate ice cream with fudge sauce and whipped cream; lemon meringue pie; homemade carrot cake with a miniature marzipan carrot in the center. So many choices that fit our two-dollars-each allowance.

The waitress brings us each a soda with a cherry and a straw. A cup of coffee for Mom. Everyone is on their best behavior. We tuck into our Easter treats taking teeny small bites, making them last. These events are never done in a hurry. They are moments to savor. She is teaching us to stop and enjoy, but I don't recognize this now.

I only know that Easter walks are divine to this girl with a sweet tooth!

* * * *

Christmas Eve, I am six years old as the snowflakes float through the air. Glittering in the street lamps, they softly land on our coats and scarves as we walk the four blocks to midnight Mass. Snow dusts the sidewalks as I march along leaving footprints. Snow is a rarity in Clarkston where we live. Snow on Christmas Eve as we walk to midnight Mass is a glorious wonder. There are no cars, just us on this sidewalk.

"Listen!" she whispers. "Listen to the snowflakes as they fall." I hear them; snowflakes singing as they float past my little ears. Christmas Eve brings magic snowflakes as we walk.

* * * *

The swimming pool in Clarkston is my summer haven. I have a swimming pool pass and a new pink two-piece bathing suit, a gift from my Dad for my May birthday. I am ten years old. Mom walks us all the mile or so from the housing projects to the community pool where I take lessons. Time flies when we walk. It never seems far. We laugh and talk, sing and giggle. The time with her is precious. She watches and cheers as I learn to dive from the low board. The other kids run through park sprinklers, jetting sprays of cold water on hot little bodies. Maybe on the way home a multicolored Rocket Popsicle from Community Foods, if we are lucky. We walk home exhausted, cooled down from the summer heat, happy.

* * * *

Christmastime 1969. This is our first Christmas away from the housing projects. Our first Christmas in a real house. I am ecstatic at eleven years old. Our new beginnings are underway. The tree is larger. Our living room, a long rectangular shape with high ceilings, is larger. The Christmas tree this year touches the ceiling! Everything is bigger and better this Christmas!

Our living room windows span the length of the room; more room for the delicate paper cut-out snowflakes we make each year. Tradition. Part of our Christmas preparations; part of keeping five kids occupied as the frenetic pace of moving toward a holiday takes hold.

In Port Angeles, where we now live, there is the upper portion of town, neighborhoods and businesses, but definitely the residential area for the city. And a there is a lower area, near the waterfront. The downtown core sits in this waterfront lower zone along the Strait of Juan de Fuca. The town is bordered on one side by the waters of the strait, with the City of Victoria, British Columbia, Canada, only eighteen miles away on the other side, and the snow-capped peaks of the Olympic Mountains protecting it from the south. Of all the places in the State of Washington Mom may have had a chance to take her first teaching post, this has to be the most incredible in terms of scenery.

The walking is slow, a gentle slope uphill throughout the overall town. And, from the neighborhoods above to the downtown businesses, one can walk down Lincoln Street, or take a set of stairs at the base of Laurel Street, or walk down a zig-zagged boardwalk, planked for easy footing; no slipping. The 'ZigZag' as it is called is at the base of Oak Street. The ZigZag is our walking route to what is downtown Port Angeles in 1969.

This year we are making a family Christmas shopping trip. Mom and five young ones on an expedition to the 88¢ Store—Roscoe's 88¢ Store to be exact. We each have a dollar and have drawn a name among ourselves, us five. Our job: think seriously about what the gift should be. What would that sibling like, and use your dollar to buy the best-suited gift. At the 88¢ Store, there are plenty of options.

Tonight's expedition is our opportunity to see what treasures are on offer for our dollar allowance. Five of us, learning to give to each other, choose something special for another. It is also five more gifts under the tree creating the anticipated Christmas morning wonder.

How Mom has managed to stash away any extra money at this time of year is beyond me. We are still using food stamps and greatly appreciate the local Catholic church for helping with holiday meals. The end of each month (teachers are paid once a month near the beginning) is a huge financial challenge. Pancakes for dinner is pretty normal fare.

But, she has done it—saved some Christmas money for us kids to use in shopping, and we have walked along Cherry street, crossing to Oak, in the early winter evening hours. Singing Christmas carols and chattering away on our shopping extravaganza, Mary in her stroller, the rest of us holding hands, staying near.

The aroma of freshly popped popcorn wafts out to First Street as we open the brightly lit doors. A string of holiday bells tinkled against the glass as five chilly little children are ushered into the warmth of the store. Candy canes ring the counters, gold-foiled wrapped boxes of holiday treats tempt shoppers as they leave.

"Oh come on. One more small gift. Take me, you know you want to!" they shout from their artfully balanced stacks.

Roscoe's 88¢ Store feels immense. Every conceivable need or desire has a place here. Bolts of brilliantly colored fabric lay atop tables at the entry. Shelf upon shelf of kitchen utensils, embroidered aprons, dishtowels and mixing bowls. Spinning racks of jackets and jeans, tee shirts and sweaters for the whole family stand closely packed together. Undies and pj's, bath towels and sheets, colored glassware for fancy table settings and placemats with scenes from around the world: The Eiffel Tower, Big Ben, Neuschwanstein Castle...placemats can take you on a journey!

Makeup! Fruit-flavored lip glosses, shiny powder compacts by CoverGirl, Maybelline and Revlon (I can hardly wait until I get to use these) and blush! Rosy, coral, tan...which one will be right for me? Sparkling hair clips, ponytail bands, and bandeaus. I am in preteen heaven!

Binders, pencils, and reams of school paper. Skip this row! Household cleaning supplies, toothpaste and deodorant, mousetraps, bug spray, and weed killer. Skip these rows!

Fairy Princess paper dolls, thick, fat wonderful coloring books with page after page of Barbie, Ken and Chrissy to color, twenty-four box sets of Crayolas (how I love periwinkle), watercolor paint sets, multicolored thin-tipped marking pens, sticker books, and story books—this is the row!

There are games galore: Chinese checkers, Go Fish cards, tic tac toe boards and jumping ropes. Matchbox cars for Joel, Barbie's newest latest outfit for Annie, scissors, glitter tubes and multicolored construction paper for Jeannie—everything is here.

And I, I have my youngest sister Mary's name. I will choose a gift for her. She is three years old. The youngest in this brood of five. Too young for the games we more grown up kids play, she needs something special; a gift that will seem BIG to little eyes. A gift that will be all hers and not to share (we share a great deal- as large families do). And there it is!

Across the aisle, on the bottom shelf, sits a child-sized chair. A chair small enough to sit at a little girl's' tea party table.

The small seat is woven rattan. A brightly painted wood frame boasts brilliant colors: poppy reds, sun-kissed lemon yellows, and a splash of royal blue. A perfect size for Mary. I know I have found the gift of the season! And, after young years learning to make the most with what we have, I recognize the value of this 88¢ Store gift, knowing I have found a deal, knowing Mom will be proud! I have chosen wisely.

We have been wandering the aisles gazing and wishing, sharing our most coveted desires with each other. Normally hands are in pockets or behind our backs. I have Annie and Jeannie with me, holding hands. We are the oldest three. Mom has Mary seated in the cart and Joel at her side, holding tight to the shopping cart, as we walk the Christmas fantasy aisles.

Taking turns, she takes each of the younger ones to collect the gifts they chose for their sibling and brings them to the counter.

"Shhh, don't tell what it is. This is a surprise for Christmas!"

I stand watch over the others as this process goes through the chain: Annie, Jeannie, Joel and Mary. When everyone's special gifts have been collected, paid for and bagged (no one must peek!), she takes them outside while I run back to collect the magnificently painted chair; the perfect gift!

Oh no! We are walking. I won't be able to carry it home; it is too far! I won't have free hands to hold hands with my sisters and brother. The chair! I have to have that chair.

Seeing my distraught face the sales clerk asks, "What's the trouble, sweetie?" When I tell her and point at Mom and my siblings outside, explain we are walking tonight, she takes over. A brief chat with Mom and she comes back to tell me she will hold the chair until tomorrow. Mom has said she will bring me down after school to pick it up. No worries, no problems! It is a lovely gift and she will make sure it is here for me. Smiling, saying my thank-yous, I am out the door.

Back to the corner we walk, the other packages tucked safely away from prying eyes under the stroller seat. And up the ZigZag. Brightly lit in the evening hours, we take turns running ahead, section by section, but not too far, as Mom pushes Mary's stroller up the boardwalk. At the top, she gathers us together for a rest— and a surprise. POPCORN! Store popcorn. It always tastes so much better than at home!

Slowly we make our way home, passing houses now lit in the dark with their Christmas finery. Lights twinkling, brilliant trees flashing in the windows of the homes we pass. We are walking in a fairyland. Excited, singing and laughing we hold hands; we talk of Christmas magic.

We walk. We share. We love.

CHAPTER FOURTEEN

Doorstopper Cookies!

"...and what have you learned?" asked the Universe.
"I am capable," answered an assured Me.

Breakfast is not yet on the tables when I venture out at 6:45 AM in search of morning coffee. No matter, coffee is all I need at this hour. Last night's meal was hearty and filling. Two evenings in a row and I have eaten like a queen in hiking and refugio standards. If I don't eat for a couple of hours, no harm done.

Lexy Ann, one of the lucky bottom bunk recipients on our room, raises a sleepy head as I sneak back to gather my belongings. My coffee waits on a table in the dining hall; this is where I will pull on boots and finish getting ready for my day. I reach over and she grabs my hand in a tight squeeze. We say our good-byes, wish each other everything wonderful and good in life and I tiptoe away.

Lexy Ann, so many aspects of this wonderful young woman remind me of an earlier Kate—a Kate of many years passed. So much reminds me of who I wish I could have been: the confidence to seek adventure at a younger age; the natural flow of conversation with everyone she meets; her willingness to let go and trust that if she follows her heart, listens to her soul, and follows her passion, all will be well. She is wise beyond her years.

* * * *

Seven-thirty AM and I am the only one on the trail as I walk away from Refugio Grey. Others are just moving, enjoying a leisurely breakfast. Obviously, those also planning to catch the 12:30 PM ferry are not fearing a challenging walk back.

Actually, the seclusion is perfection on this morning in Torres del Paine National Park. Although on a timetable, I have allotted time for a relaxed hike back, even if the boulder barrier causes a temporary slowdown.

Remarkably, when I approach my nemesis thirty minutes later, I find, as always, the climbing up is far easier than the coming down. A few moments of calculated planning as I stand gazing at the granite wall of boulders before me: place my foot there, pull up with my right hand on that rock sticking out, move the other foot up and in a tad, grab that bush branch with my left hand, do it again twice more and I will be at the top! Problem solved. Up I go, laughing at my slightly goofy looking ascent. Laughing even more when I straighten up on top and catch the eyes of the two guys below me watching this morning's cartoon show.

"Quite the show, huh?" I grin as they ascend the boulders.

"Hey, you did it! That's all that matters!" They give me a quick round of applause and head on their way.

The morning flies by. Clear blue skies, a gentle breeze whistling from the rock faces of the massif high above, an occasional crack echoing across the valley as Glacier Grey carves new icebergs into the lake...a miracle of a morning. Birds twitter loudly and I realize that in the rush of the winds yesterday I had not heard them, had not even seen them.

The mirador of Lago Grey is where I stop for a bite to eat. Icebergs in the lake that yesterday stunned me with their gemstone blues shades, once again give me pause to take a deep breath of wonder as I find a quiet corner to settle in for a morning snack.

Having left as early as I did today, I walked away from a breakfast, likely oatmeal, as well as the complimentary lunch sack I have received each day as part of the accommodation package I purchased for this trip. Tucked in my backpack are leftover nibbles from the last couple of days: an apple, a juice box, the mandatory granola bar, and a couple of three-day-old cookies. Plenty for a mid-morning breakfast extravaganza!

Opening the tin foil pack my cookies have called home (everything in lunches has been wrapped in tin foil up here), I am looking forward to a bite of something sweet this morning. Perhaps my reward for having climbed the boulder barrier without falling on my face! Perhaps because I am feeling pretty proud of myself for having made this trek, NOTHING I have ever done before. Or perhaps just because I have a sweet tooth! Whatever the case, the cookies are a well-earned reward.

Until I bite into the first one. Thick, rich looking homemade chocolate cookies with not an ounce of give. They won't break. They don't crumble! Gnawing the edges of these little darlings will be the only way to savor what I can tell is lovely flavor; they are just rock hard.

Oh my God, here I am in Patagonian Chile and I have *Doorstopper Cookies* for my breakfast. Ohhhh my God...I am laughing as the tears flow.

Learning to bake was a sacred rite of passage in our house. At least it seemed that way to me. Why the intense desire to learn I am not quite sure, I only know that the chance to bake could not come soon enough. Most likely, now that I think on it as an adult, it is because as a young girl with an insatiable sweet tooth, if I learn to bake cookies for our lunch sacks, then I also had the enviable right to taste the dough, lick the batter bowl, and sneak the first cookie from the oven. I made them, I taste them, right?

Whatever the draw, I first got to bake at age eleven.

Rule of thumb: FIRST, you have to be tall enough to easily reach over the electric burners on the stovetop, to the knobs along the back face. Four coiled burners are the barrier between me and learning to bake.

And, her orders are "easily reach over" which means no tippy toes and no jumping; arms must be well above the burner surfaces. No accidental burns allowed. Once able to meet this first criteria, all knobs and dials must be explained to Mom, in a clear and concise fashion. She is adamant that complete comprehension of the operation of the stove and oven has to be achieved; she will consider my being allowed to bake only when she trusts I understand.

"See, I can reach the ones for the oven just fine. First I turn this one to BAKE and then I turn the temperature to 350 degrees. That's what the recipe says."

Smiling as I glance over at her, I know I am on track to pass test number one.

"This is the timer. After I put the pan in the oven, I will set the timer for eleven minutes. While the cookies are baking the oven door stays closed."

"What are those other dials for, Kathy? Explain which one is which." She wants one hundred percent clarity.

She called me Kathy more often that Katy. I was, am, her Kathy-girl. Katy had been bestowed upon me by my Grandma Meyers, her Mother, and it stuck. To my Grandma and Grandpa, I was Katy, to my siblings I was Katy—unless of course I was 'Bossy Katy,' which I did deserve at times, I admit. And, to my Mom I was Katy, at times, but today I am Kathy. Today, in the heart of a lesson and in showing that I am responsible enough to venture forth and bake a batch of cookies on my own, I am Kathy. Kathy is responsible.

"Well, this one on top is for the back burner here, the left, and this one on the bottom in for the front. Over here, the one on top is for this right back burner, and this one on the bottom is for the front. Right?"

"Right! And do you need those burners to make your cookies?" she asks.

"No, don't need them."

"Good, then don't touch them," she smiles.

The First stage has been completed and I have passed with flying colors. NOW comes the tough part in the "Now you are Old enough, Tall enough, and Smart enough to Learn to Bake' test in the Elliott household It is time to read and fully explain each step of the Old Fashioned Rolled Sugar Cookie Recipe.

Now, that may sound rather simplistic. What's so tough about a sugar cookie recipe? Well, in our old red and white, edges bent a bit, Betty Crocker Cookbook, the one used for absolutely everything which needs a cookbook as I am growing up, the Old Fashioned Rolled Sugar Cookie Recipe is extremely detailed.

Not only does it involve more than three to four ingredients, it calls for their proportioning down to an eighth of a teaspoon. There isn't even an eighth of a teaspoon spoon on the ring! The recipe details mixing instructions, ingredient by ingredient, and the patting of the dough into segments to be refrigerated for an hour to obtain the right consistency for rolling with the rolling pin, and cutting with a multitude of well-used tin cookie cutters. It explains flouring the surface of a breadboard or counter to keep the dough from sticking. The baking sheets are to be lightly greased and the cookies, once cut, brushed with an egg white wash so multicolored sugar sprinkles will adhere. It is a very detailed recipe for an eleven-year-old out to prove herself in the baking arena for the very first time.

And, this detailed recipe must be read and explained to Mom in a convincing enough fashion that she knows, beyond a shadow of a doubt, I have full comprehension of the steps involved in baking Old Fashioned Rolled Sugar Cookies. She will check in while my project is underway, but this my baking challenge. I will do this one myself!

Having mastered the test, I am allowed to set out on a Saturday afternoon, her apron wrapped tight around my waist, ingredients all lined out on the counter for easy access, and concoct my first batch of Old Fashioned Rolled Sugar Cookies.

I get overly enthusiastic sometimes when getting to finally do what I want. Some kids, learning a new skill, move through processes slowly and deliberately, enjoying each step of the way, savoring the journey. Although I'll reach that phase much later in my life, at eleven years old, I am a speed demon when it comes to getting things done. Fast is good. Fast means I understand. Fast shows I am smart! That's my belief system at eleven years old.

How or why the necessary amount, in teaspoons, of baking soda and baking powder requirements get mixed with Tablespoons when entering the mix, I don't know. But it happens.

Completely confident I trust everything is going perfectly as I move through the rolling of the dough, the placement of cookie cutter cut-outs and the reuse of dough edges left to the wayside. Gather it up and mix in with the next batch I roll flat. I monitor the baking time to a tee. I am so proud of this masterful accomplishment and excited to bite into these yummy sugary tasting treats.

One minute left. Buzzzzzz goes the oven timer. Opening the oven door, a blast of heat fogs my glasses forcing my head back until they clear.

Ohhhhh, the cookies look too brown on the edges. My beautiful perfect cut-outs are slightly burned. I take the pan out, placing it to cool on a oven mitt placed on the counter for just this purpose.

The second pan of cookies is already to go into the oven. Mom has been checking in and suggested that I have baking pan number two ready when baking pan number one comes out so as to keep the process rolling—lessons in efficiency. In it goes.

A few minutes of cooling time and the first batch of cookies is lifted one by one from the pan onto a plate. Not exactly the pretty cookies I see in magazines, I am sure they will taste divine anyway. How can anything sweet not taste divine?

Time for the first bite! I bite down on my carefully crafted cookie only to have it remain solid against my teeth. My confection of sweet, yummy butter and vanilla flavoring does not easily fall apart on my tongue, sugar sweet goodness melting in my mouth. What's wrong? My cookie is rock hard—literally, rock hard! I try again. A solid mass of nonedible cookie.

"Mom!" "What's wrong? My cookies. I followed the recipe. I know I did. I did it exactly as it says!" I argue as she picks up a cookie and attempts to take a bite. No go.

"Katy, honey, you must have missed something in the recipe. They would not be like this if they had been done just like the recipe calls for."

"But I did; I did follow it exactly. I know I did!" I am a stubborn eleven-year-old, so damned sure of myself.

"Honey, no. Something is wrong with the mix. You made a mistake. It's okay. It happens." She is starting to smile as she surveys the floured counter top and a sink full of mixing utensils.

"They taste okay sweetie, they are just hard, that's all. We will dip them in milk and they will be just fine. You'll see. Go ahead, finish the rest. Let's not waste the dough. You can finish them without rolling them out. Just plop a spoonful on the pan and flatten it with a fork, see?"

She is right. No sense wasting time rolling and cutting hard as rock cookies that are going to get soaked in milk and fall apart anyway. Stupid me! My project, therefore my responsibility to finish what I started. I pushed for this rite of passage, I must see it through.

What is truly remarkably, amazingly wonderful about my Mom is that even when everything seems to be going to hell in a handbasket—and for me it feels that way this Saturday afternoon of my first baking adventure—she looks to find humor and encourages each of us kids to see the humor in situations as well.

"Always keep your sense of humor. You have to able to laugh! You can handle anything in life if you can laugh!!"

She has held that motto all our lives. Even in the midst of this sugar cookie tragedy she is able to get us, me and my siblings who have come in for a taste for Katy's first baking extravaganza, giggling.

The final batches are solid, granite consistency, chunks. Sweet, and yes, they will soften in milk, if we wait...a few minutes. We are laughing hysterically by now. Besides dipping them in milk and eating them that way, what good are they? We start a game. Who can come up with the most outlandish uses for rock hard sugar cookies?

Now it is funny. Now it doesn't matter that my first foray into the baking world has gone awry. We are all six together in the kitchen giggling and teasing each other as we shout out crazy ideas.

She has done this. She has, as only Mom can do, made a game and a memory.

"I know," shouts my younger sister Annie, laughing so hard her little mouth aches as she grabs her cheeks and squeezes them together to stop her spreading smile.

"We can use them as doorstoppers, see?" She runs to the kitchen door, elaborately placing a chunk of cookie between the door and the frame, then giving the door a solid shove. Bang! It stops hard against the nugget.

Tears are rolling as we double over, laughing hysterically at her antics.

"DOORSTOPPER COOKIES!"

And she is right. My first long-awaited baking experiment, the one I begged for and proved myself ready to handle, is now one for the family lore. Doorstopper Cookies they are!

OH they are going to howl when they hear about this. Chocolate *Doorstopper Cookies,* somewhere in the mountains of Patagonia!

The last of my apple gone, I pack up tin foil, doorstopper cookies, and the apple core, and strap on my backpack for a last hike out of the mountains. Glorious. The remainder of the walk is nothing short of stunningly, beautifully, incredibly, mystically, glorious.

Two hours later and I am entering Paine Grande campground and my completion of the W Trek. Poles in the air, grin on my face, others that have walked into the 'end zone' ahead of me cheer me on. There are five of us gathered together, shooting the perfunctory

"I am HERE. I MADE it!" photos against the backdrop of the Chilean national flag. Laughing as we relish this moment of accomplishment, myself and four other women I have never met, agree a cold cerveza is in order and head to the mini-grocery which services the facility.

An hour later, our ferry pulls in, loading well over one hundred trekkers who have made their way to the docks on this final phase of the circuit. A thirty-minute ride across the calm blue waters of Lake Pehoe takes us back to the park station where shuttle busses will whisk us to the National Park Headquarters at the park entry. Here is where my several hour return bus trip to El Calafate will begin, the final transfer taking place once past the chaotic customs and immigration station marking the boundaries of Chile and Argentina.

* * * *

Ventricular clouds, golden in hue, float against an indigo sky. The steppe stretches as far as my eyes will focus. The bus is eerily quiet except for the constant hum of a tired engine.

Hikers and day-trippers, heads nodding at bumps in the road, sleep away these final hours into El Calafate. I am left alone with my thoughts; left alone to consider what lies ahead when the next couple of days have passed and a plane will whisk me back to the States.

This Patagonian adventure was to be my proof that I had the skills and the heart to take on the Via Francigena. A more than two thousand-kilometer pilgrimage trail from Canterbury England to the heart of Christianity in Rome, the VF walk has been calling to me since the end of my Spanish Camino.

Now, after the W Trek, I am certain in my abilities; it is just a matter of setting the dates. But first, a walk in the Scottish Highlands with friend Helen, planned for May, three months from now. There is no reason I could not simply choose to stay in Europe and begin the Via Francigena once we have completed the West Highland Way. Perfect!

The VF will take three full months and summer walking allows for little concern of snow while crossing the Alps at the Gran San Bernard Pass in Switzerland. Then the path winds south through northwestern Italy, traversing the Tuscan countryside and south to Rome. I can do this! I have the time before rejoining the workforce in the next year. This is the time; do it NOW!

A calm sense of 'this is right; this is the next phase' settles my brain, quiets my heart. The decision is made. I drift off, head nodding with the others.

CHAPTER FIFTEEN

Going Home!

"Are you ready to go home? asked the Universe.
"I am home," smiled a contented Me.

Our bus arrives late in the evening to a quiet El Calafate. Due back at around 8:00 PM, it is now 10:30 PM as we pull up in front of the hotel. In the morning a shuttle, arranged for 7:00 AM, will take me to the local airport where my multi-leg flight home to Seattle will commence. A short night is in store as I know there will be a plethora of emails to scan, as well as several to be written letting family know all is well and I am on my way.

When I began this adventure, I knew I would have internet access at two of the refugios on the W Trek. Well, I assumed I would have internet as it was mentioned in their website information. What I did not realize is that although internet may be available, it was *not* available to guests. Limited connectivity kept internet usage for the refugio service staff and emergencies. Makes sense. That my family has not heard from me in six days, however, is not good. Connecting tonight and ensuring everyone that their crazy, wandering mother/sister/daughter is alive and well is paramount.

Sure enough, a quick scan of waiting messages, and I am keenly aware I have an alarmed family. Messages, email, and Facebook, from my Mom and sisters are troubled, worried.

My son's note, bless him, is straightforward:

"Mom, I know you are okay. I would feel it if you weren't. But, Grandma and Aunty Mary are worried. Call or write them as soon as you see this! Then write me. I love You. Greg." That he has known since he was young he would feel if anything was ever wrong with me is a testament to his, perhaps other than consciously, recognition that we are energetically connected, always.

The next hour or more is spent with brief messages and Facebook chats letting everyone know all is well, and tomorrow I will head for home.

"Yes, I know, I thought there would be internet and I am so, so sorry to have worried you. I KNOW the information says it will be available, but it was not. You called to find me? Oh my God, I feel terrible. They said I had already left? You called my hotel here in El Calafate too?

Yes, yes, I was told I would be moved to a different hotel when I got back as they were oversold. Nice thing is I got upgraded to the best in town. Yes, that's where I am now. I love you...I am so sorry you worried!"

My poor family; my poor Mom. But now, everyone knows I am safe and sound. No broken bones, no major mishaps. And it is midnight. Some repacking for the plane, a long hot shower, and a few hours sleep. Tomorrow—home!

* * * *

My travels take me from El Calafate Airport into Buenos Aires. Busses are available to transport travelers from the national airport, which I fly into, to the international airport some forty-five to sixty minutes away depending on traffic. Today the traffic is easy and we arrive at Ezeiza International Airport with three hours until my next flight.

At JFK International in New York, I will have five hours before my flight to Seattle. Normally a layover such as this, on a twenty-four-hour travel day, would be a huge frustration. However, today it allows for a lunch visit with friend Desi who moved to the East Coast two years ago. A bus from Connecticut, where she lives, will bring her to Grand Central Station in New York and she will hop the train to JFK so we have some hug and chat time. Excited to see a friend I have not seen in several years, I am truly grateful that she will commute all this way to spend time with me. Blessed; that is the word. I am blessed and grateful for a long layover!

Family and friendships take nurturing for relationships to remain strong. For some, yes, it can be months with little or no contact; picking up right where you left off seems natural. Those relationships are forged in unconditional love and they are few and far between. And even then, I am of the belief that when you care about someone, friend or family, connection is everything. Staying in touch on a regular basis is vitally important for both parties.

Perhaps six years living overseas convinced me even more of this truth. Accused of spending far too much time facing west from my home in Spain, to have abandoned my innate desire to nurture my friendships at home and ensure my family knew I was only a phone call or email away, would have gone against everything I believe about loving friends and family and what that looks like.

Now, comfy in my aisle, Delta Airlines Economy Comfort seat thirty-three thousand feet in the air, I am on the final leg of my flight home to the Pacific Northwest. My flight home to what will be a new life. Contemplating the last two and half weeks I recognize the miracle of my hike in Patagonia.

That days in the glories of a land I had dreamed of since my teen years would have been spent drifting to memories of home and childhood, memories of Mom and all she created in my happiest of remembrances, was nothing I could have anticipated.

Mary Jo, walking with me as I came down that last steep path into los Cuernos, staying with me throughout the remainder of the hike, to rejoice in the wonder of again sharing a remarkable experience together, was a gift. A blessed reminder that I am connected if I stay open and allow myself to listen.

Sounds, nature noises, and photographic images I never before paid attention to hearing or seeing, play in a loop on the tape in my head:

Caterpillars, dozens and dozens of them, slowly slinking across dirt trails

Trees bending in the wind, their creaking the 'caw- caw' of exotic birds

Heart-shaped rocks giving pause for gratitude stops; a prayer for a friend or family member with each one found

Clouds shifting so quickly over Mount Fitz Roy and Cerro Torres. One moment these remarkable peaks magnificent in their splendor, the next erased in mist of clouds

The craggy saw-toothed blade peaks of los Cuernos slicing the sky

CRACK! BOOM! as the glacier calves into Lago Grey

Bent windblown trees, doubled over in their tired fight against the raging Patagonian winds

Earth, the rich musty smell of the dirt as a summer rain pummels dry trails

Winds howling through ancient canyons; ghosts gathering in the mountains

How odd that I grew up on the doorstep of the enchanting Olympic National Park, the Olympic Mountains, and yet until now, until Patagonia, did not appreciate these magnificent treasures.

Going home. I am going home.

How do I feel? Serene. Ready? Yes, ready.

On the return from Spain, from the Camino this last fall, the *going home* produced anxiety, concern over facing a new life in an old world. Three months later—it has only been three months—and I know my future will be bright. I trust that all is in order and will show itself to me when I need to see. The Universe conspires on my behalf when I simply state my intentions and move forward with trust.

Nothing in my life is out of order!

What is called on, from me, is to remain open.

Watch for the synchronicities given as guidance, trust they are there. Listen and watch for angel messages as they come my way. Jeannie, Sis, and MJ are with me each and every day. Pay attention to the call of my soul and what brings joy and peace to my heart. Remain grateful for all I have and all I will have. Grateful for the blessings in life; grateful for friends and family who love me and who I love beyond all else. And, grateful for this amazing South American adventure. It has brought me full circle. It has brought me home.

EPILOGUE

In May 2015, three months after my trek in Patagonia, I ventured to Scotland with a lifelong friend, Helen, to walk the West Highland Way. We had planned this mixed Scottish adventure, part hike, part Scotch whiskey tour, several months prior.

Upon completion of this hike, my plan was to stay in Europe and take on the Via Francigena, The itinerary I planned to follow would take slightly more than three months; three months walking on my own through the countryside of Western Europe.

Life can be cruelly unfair. Why certain people become ill with cancer when their life patterns were healthy makes no sense. When cancer is not a genetic variable, why should it happen? In April 2015, my son learned that his father, a man I had loved and married during my twenties, was facing terminal cancer. The doctor's decree: four to six months at most.

My son Greg is my only child. Twenty-nine years old when he received this news, he is still my baby boy. My babe facing the loss of his father, a Dad who loved him beyond measure. A Dad who would give his life for his boy. A Dad who would become Greg's dear and true friend as he grew into manhood.

My place was home, close to my son when he needed me, not trekking across the mountains of Switzerland!

Plans were adjusted to ensure I was close at hand as Gary became more ill. Helen and I would go to Scotland, hike our planned adventure. I would then fly to Florence and proceed with a section of the Via Francigena; a section taking only two weeks. My timetable: back in Seattle late June.

Another oncologist appointment and the window of time has now been shortened. Helen and I are already in Scotland on the first leg of our trip; the tourist leg. The hike will commence in a couple more days. It is clear that the Via Francigena will have to wait for another time. Airlines tickets are adjusted, and I plan to fly home immediately upon completion of our hike at the first of June, three weeks from now.

May 17th. We are scheduled to start the hike the next day, a hike that will have us in rural Scotland and, except for the evening hours at our hotels, virtually out of phone contact. Greg and I connect on Facebook as he wishes me an early birthday message— my birthday is the 18th. I let him know I am now due home June 2nd.

"Mom, I doubt he will make it that long."

My heart breaks for my boy. And, as I look back, how incredible the Universe. A day later and reaching us would have been far more difficult; getting to an airport even more so. On this night a new decision is made.

The next day, Helen and I train to Inverness where we can catch flights to Amsterdam the following morning. She will stay with friends until her planned return to the States and I will fly directly to Seattle, as quickly as possible. The West Highland Way will wait for another day. It will be there.

On the flight home from Patagonia, I knew without question I was headed exactly where I was meant to be. At the time, being with my son as he faced his father's death was in no way what I might have conceived of as my *why*. Over a year later, I am forever grateful to have been close —to call Seattle home—rather than far away Spain. I am where I am meant to be; all is in order. Nothing in my life is out of order!

Greg's Dad died June 10th of that year. He died bravely, offering a laugh whenever he could, and providing love to his family until the final moments.

As for me, I spent the summer of 2015 working on my first book. A writer's conference in March of 2015, immediately following my return from Patagonia, called to me. Emails from Hay House Publications, the publishing company which published for my favorite authors, Dr. Wayne Dyer, Gregg Braden, and Anita Moorjani, kept pinging my in-box. Intrigued, the message to attend was clear to my heart and I signed up and attended.

Following and trusting. That March conference laid the groundwork for what would finally become *A Camino of the Soul: Learning to Listen When the Universe Whispers.* The work of that summer of 2015, although cathartic in dealing with the end of my marriage, became far too detailed in the nitty gritty of a relationship capsized. What would finally emerge in the spring of this year 2016, is a work I am proud to call my first book.

In September of 2015, I did hike a portion of the Via Francigena with a hiking partner. We walked from Lucca to Rome through the heart of Tuscany. Truly remarkably, beautiful, inspirational...the Via calls me to return. I will one day!

Next up: September 2016 Camino Portuguese. Over six hundred kilometers from Lisbon, Portugal to Santiago de Compostela in Spain. This one I will walk alone.

What will come I have no idea. I just know I am meant to do this one alone, connected to whatever the Universe brings my way, and I cannot wait to find out!

Wait and watch. Book #3 is in the making!

AUTHOR BIO

Katharine Elliott left a successful thirty-year career in the hospitality industry to care for her mother-in-law as she fought her last months of a fifteen-year battle with cancer. Within two weeks of her death, Kate's middle sister was diagnosed with pancreatic cancer. Four and a half months later, she took her last breath.

After the deaths, she and her husband made a bold move, followed their hearts and settled overseas to live a dream in Europe. They spent four years in a medieval Croatian village on the Adriatic, followed by a move to the Costa Blanca in Spain. In the summer of 2011, Katharine read and reread authors Wayne Dyer, Anita Moorjani, and Paulo Coelho. Focused on a new way of thinking, she embarked on a path of spiritual growth.

Following her soul's calling, Katharine walked the eight-hundred-kilometer Camino Santiago de Compostela in the fall of 2014. That journey sparked a passion for long-distance walking and a call to write. In February 2015, Katharine hiked the famed W Trek of Patagonian Chile and the renowned trails of

Argentina's El Chaltén. Her next walk took her to Italy in September 2015, to trek a portion of the Via Francigena, a pilgrimage of approximately two thousand kilometers stretching from Canterbury to Rome.

A native of the Pacific Northwest, Katharine attended Portland Community College and Portland State, studying Speech Communication and Public speaking. Katharine has one son, Gregory, a daughter-in-law, Allison, and granddaughter, Gwen Dylan Rose. Katharine's large extended family lives in the Pacific Northwest.

A Heartfelt Thank-You

Thank-you for choosing to buy and read *Patagonia - the Camino Home*.

As a self-published author, having reviews posted via Amazon is essential to the success of the book.

Thank-you so much for taking a couple minutes and sharing your thoughts. Just log onto Amazon, type *Patagonia - the Camino Home* in the SEARCH bar, and you will be directed to my page. From there simply click the "Write a Review" link and you are set.

With gratitude,

Katharine

Made in the USA
San Bernardino, CA
08 December 2016